The Essence of David Hume

The Essence of David Hume

On Religion, Morals, and Economics

Edited by

Henry Lewis & Hunter Lewis

with Introductions by

Hunter Lewis

The Essence of . . . series of books are edited versions of great works of moral philosophy, distilled to reveal the essence of their authors' thought and argument. To read the complete, unedited version of this work, and see the excised passages, please visit our website at www.AxiosInstitute.org.

Axios Press
PO Box 457
Edinburg, VA 22824
888.542.9467   info@axiosinstitute.org

Library of Congress Cataloging-in-Publication Data

The essence of David Hume : on religion, morals, and economics / edited by Henry Lewis & Hunter Lewis ; with Introductions by Hunter Lewis.
    pages cm. -- (The essence of-- series)
    Includes bibliographical references and index.
    ISBN 978-1-60419-090-8 (pbk. : alk. paper) 1. Hume, David, 1711-1776.
    I. Lewis, Henry, 1996- editor.

B1498.E87 2014

192--dc23

2014027576

Contents

Part Two: Morals

Part Three: Economics

Part Four: Life

Part One

Religion

Introduction

IF ANYBODY QUALIFIES as a secular saint, it must surely be Scottish philosopher David Hume (1711–1776). Secular certainly describes him: he regarded religion as the supreme source of both superstition and fanaticism, the twin evils which bedeviled and enslaved the human mind.

That he was saint-like in his personal life may be more arguable, but there is plenty of evidence for it. Here is Hume's description of himself, an account that was verified by everyone who knew him:

> ... I possess the same ardor as ever in study, and the same gaiety in company.... It is difficult to be more detached from life than I am at present....

> ... I was, I say, a man of mild dispositions, of command of temper, of an open, social,

and cheerful humor, capable of attachment, but little susceptible of enmity, and
of great moderation in all my passions.…
("My Own Life")

His close friend Adam Smith, the great economist,
witnessed his stoic and uncomplaining acceptance of
death, as diarrhea steadily robbed him of strength,
and on his passing wrote the following to Hume's publisher and friend William Strahan:

Thus died our most excellent, and never to
be forgotten friend; concerning whose …
character and conduct there can scarce be a
difference of opinion. His temper, indeed,
seemed to be more happily balanced, if I
may be allowed such an expression, than
that perhaps of any other man I have ever
known.… The extreme gentleness of his
nature never weakened … the steadiness of
his resolutions. His constant pleasantry was
the genuine effusion of good-nature and
good-humor, tempered with delicacy and
modesty, and without even the slightest
tincture of malignity.… Upon the whole,
I have always considered him, both in his
lifetime and since his death, as approaching as nearly to the idea of a perfectly wise
and virtuous man, as perhaps the nature

of human frailty will permit. (Letter from
Adam Smith to William Strahan)

As amiable, lovable, and serene as Hume always
seemed to appear to his friends, he was also fully human.
This is how the youthful Hume described himself in
his first book:

> ... I have exposed myself to the enmity of
> all metaphysicians, logicians, mathemati-
> cians, and even theologians. . . . When I
> look abroad, I foresee on every side, dis-
> pute, contradiction, anger, calumny and
> detraction. When I turn my eye inward, I
> find nothing but doubt and ignorance. . . .
>
> Most fortunately it happens, that since rea-
> son is incapable of dispelling these clouds,
> nature herself suffices to that purpose, and
> cures me of this philosophical melancholy
> and delirium, either by relaxing this bent
> of mind, or by some avocation, and lively
> impression of my senses, which obliterate
> all these chimeras. I dine, I play a game of
> backgammon, I converse, and am merry
> with my friends. . . .
>
> [Even so], I make bold to recommend phi-
> losophy, and shall not scruple to give it the
> preference to superstition of every kind or

denomination.... The [ancient Greek] Cynics are an extraordinary instance of philosophers, who from reasonings purely philosophical ran into as great extravagancies of conduct as any Monk or Dervish that ever was in the world. Generally speaking, the errors in religion are dangerous; those in philosophy only ridiculous.

I am sensible, that . . . there are in England, in particular, many honest gentlemen, who being always employed in their domestic affairs, or amusing themselves in common recreations, have carried their thoughts very little beyond those objects, which are every day exposed to their senses. And indeed, of such as these I pretend not to make philosophers. . . . They do well to keep themselves in their present situation; and instead of refining them into philosophers, I wish we could communicate to our founders of systems, a share of this gross earthy mixture, as an ingredient, which they commonly stand much in need of. . . . (*A Treatise of Human Nature*, Book I, Section VII)

This reflective, learned, cultivated, gentle, tolerant, calm, companionable, loyal, witty, and good man was also an implacable foe of all religion, which he considered an evil. In a letter to a friend, he referred to the realm of "Stupidity, Christianity, and Ignorance." (Hume to Hugh Blair, April 6, 1765)

Peter Gay, in his superb, two volume history of the European "Enlightenment" movement of Hume's time, mentions this letter (vol. 1, p. 20). He also recounts (vol. 1, p. 356–57) how James Boswell, Samuel Johnson's celebrated biographer and a firm Christian believer, despite his acknowledged moral lapses, visited Hume on his deathbed in a last effort to save his soul. He found Hume "lean, ghastly, and quite of an earthy appearance." When Boswell asked whether "it was not possible there might be a future state," the philosopher responded that "it was a most unreasonable fancy that he should exist forever." Boswell, thinking of "my excellent mother's pious instructions," then asked "would it not be agreeable to have hopes of seeing our friends again?" and "mentioned three men lately deceased, for whom I knew he had a high value." Hume "owned that it would be agreeable, but added that none of them entertained such a notion. I believe he said, such a foolish, or such an absurd notion. . . ." This final interview was entirely consistent with the way Hume led his entire life. The foe of Christianity, whose own personal life had been so exemplary, faced extinction with unwavering calm and courage.

Here follows a summary of his thoughts on religion:

1. Of Theology

… [The work] … of [theologians] … arise[s] either from … human vanity …, or from the craft of popular superstitions.… Chased from the open country … [of reason], these robbers fly into the forest, and lie in wait to break in upon every unguarded avenue of the mind, and overwhelm it with religious fears and prejudices. … (*An Enquiry Concerning Human Understanding*, Section I, 6)

2. Of Miracles

… As the evidence, derived from witnesses and human testimony, is founded on past experience, so it varies with the experience, and is regarded either as a *proof* or a *probability*.… The ultimate standard, by which we determine all disputes, that may arise concerning them, is always derived from experience and observation.…

A miracle is a violation of the laws of nature; … There must … be a uniform experience against every miraculous event, otherwise the event would not merit that appellation. And as a uniform experience amounts to a proof, there is here a direct and full *proof,* from the nature of the fact, against the existence of any miracle; nor can such a proof be destroyed, or the miracle rendered credible, but by an opposite proof, which is superior.

The plain consequence is (and it is a general maxim worthy of our attention), "That no testimony is sufficient to establish a miracle, unless the testimony be of such a kind, that its falsehood would be more miraculous, than the fact, which it endeavors to establish. . . ." (Ibid., Section X, Part I)

It is easy to show, that . . . there never was a miraculous event established on so full an evidence. . . . In addition, we observe . . . that . . . whatever is different is contrary; . . . all the prodigies of different religions are to be regarded as contrary facts, and the evidences of these prodigies, whether weak or strong, as opposite to each other. . . . This argument . . . is not in reality different from the reasoning of a judge, who supposes, that the credit of two witnesses, maintaining a crime against any one, is destroyed by the testimony of two others. . . .

... Let us [now] examine those miracles, related in scripture; and not to lose ourselves in too wide a field, ... confine ourselves to such as we find in the *Pentateuch*.... Here ... we ... consider a book, presented to us by a barbarous and ignorant people, ... and in all probability long after the facts which it relates, corroborated by no concurring testimony.... Upon reading this book, we find it full of prodigies and miracles. It gives an account of a state of the world and of human nature entirely different from the present: of our fall from that state; of the age of man, extended to near a thousand years; of the destruction of the world by a deluge; of the arbitrary choice of one people, as the favorites of heaven; and that people the countrymen of the author; of their deliverance from bondage by prodigies the most astonishing imaginable. I desire any one to lay his hand upon his heart, and after a serious consideration declare, whether he thinks that the falsehood of such a book, supported by such a testimony, would be more extraordinary and miraculous than all the miracles it relates. ...

We may conclude [from this], that the *Christian Religion* not only was at first attended with miracles, but even at this day cannot be believed by any reasonable person without one. Mere reason is insufficient to convince us of its veracity: and whoever is moved by *Faith* to assent to it, is conscious of a continued miracle in his own person, which subverts all the principles of his understanding, and gives him a determination to believe what is most contrary to custom and experience. (Ibid., Section X, Part II)

3. Of Religious Behavior

Celibacy, fasting, penance, mortification, self-denial, humility, silence, solitude, and the whole train of monkish virtues; for what reason are they everywhere rejected by men of sense, but because they serve no manner of purpose; neither advance a man's fortune in the world, nor render him a more valuable member of society; neither qualify him for the entertainment of company, nor increase his power of self-enjoyment? We observe, on the contrary, that they cross all these desirable ends; stupefy the understanding and harden the heart, obscure the fancy and sour the temper. We justly, therefore, transfer them to the opposite column, and place them in the catalog of vices; nor has any superstition force sufficient among men of the world, to pervert entirely these natural sentiments. A gloomy, hair-brained enthusiast, after his death, may have a place in the calendar; but will scarcely ever be admitted, when alive, into intimacy and society, except by those who are as delirious and dismal as himself. (*An Enquiry Concerning the Principles of Morals*, Section IX, Conclusion, Part I)

4. Philosophy as an Antidote to Religion

Philosophy . . . is . . . the sovereign antidote to . . . superstition and false religion. All other remedies against that pestilent distemper are vain, or, at least, uncertain. Plain good sense and the practice of the world, which alone serve most purposes of life, are here found ineffectual: History, as well as daily experience, affords instances of men, endowed with the strongest capacity for business and affairs, who have all their lives crouched under slavery to the grossest superstition. Even gaiety and sweetness of temper, which infuse a balm into every other wound, afford no remedy to so virulent a poison. . . . But when sound philosophy has once gained possession of the mind, superstition is effectually excluded; and one may safely affirm, that her triumph over this enemy is more complete than over most of the vices and imperfections, incident to human nature. Love or anger, ambition or avarice, have their root in the temper and affections, which the soundest reason is scarce ever able fully to correct. But superstition, being founded on false opinion, must immediately vanish, when true philosophy has inspired juster sentiments of superior powers. . . .

It will here be superfluous to magnify the merits of philosophy, by displaying the pernicious tendency of that vice, of which it cures the human mind. The superstitious man, says Tully [Cicero], is miserable in every scene, in every incident of life. Even sleep itself, which banishes all other cares of unhappy mortals, affords to him matter of new terror; while he examines his dreams, and finds in those visions of the night, prognostications of future calamities. ("On Suicide")

5. Of Superstition and Enthusiasm

These two species of false religion, though both pernicious, are yet of a very different, and even of a contrary nature. The mind of man is subject to certain unaccountable terrors and apprehensions.... As these enemies are entirely invisible and unknown, the methods taken to appease them are equally unaccountable, and consist in ceremonies, observances, mortifications, sacrifices, presents, or in any practice, however absurd or frivolous, which either folly or knavery recommends to a blind and terrified credulity....

But the mind of man is also subject to an unaccountable elevation and presumption.... In such a state of mind, the imagination swells with great, but confused conceptions, to which no sublunary beauties or enjoyments can correspond. Everything mortal and perishable vanishes as unworthy of attention; and a full range is given to the fancy in the invisible regions, or world of Spirits.... Hence arise raptures, transports, and surprising flights of fancy; and, confidence and presumption still increasing, these raptures, being altogether unaccountable, and seeming quite beyond the reach of our ordinary faculties, are attributed to the immediate inspiration of that Divine Being who is the object of devotion. In a little time, the inspired person comes to regard himself as a distinguished favorite of the Divinity; and when this frenzy once takes place, ... the fanatic madman delivers himself over ... to inspiration from above....

... *Religions which partake of enthusiasm, are, on their first rise, more furious and violent than those which partake of superstition; but in a little time become more gentle and moderate....* Enthusiasm produces the most cruel disorders in human society; but its fury is like that of thunder and tempest, which exhaust themselves in a little time, and leave the air more calm and serene than before.... Superstition, on the contrary, steals in gradually and insensibly; renders men tame and submissive; is acceptable to the magistrate, and seems inoffensive to the people; till at last the priest, having firmly established his authority, becomes the tyrant and disturber of human society, by his endless contentions, persecutions, and religious wars....

Superstition is [also] an enemy to civil liberty, and enthusiasm a friend to it. As superstition groans under the dominion of priests, and enthusiasm is destructive of all ecclesiastical power, this sufficiently accounts for the present observation. Not to mention that enthusiasm, being the infirmity of bold and ambitious tempers, is naturally accompanied with a spirit of liberty; as superstition, on the contrary, renders men tame and abject, and fits them for slavery.... ("Of Superstition and Enthusiasm")

6. Of an Afterlife

... There arise ... in some minds ... unaccountable terrors with regard to futurity; but these would quickly vanish were they not artificially fostered by precept and education. And those who foster them, what is their motive? Only to gain a livelihood, and to acquire power and riches in this world. Their very zeal and industry, therefore, are an argument against them.

What cruelty, what iniquity, what injustice in nature, to confine all our concern, as well as all our knowledge, to the present life, if there be another scene still waiting us of infinitely greater consequence? Ought this barbarous deceit to be ascribed to a beneficent and wise being? . . . ,

Punishment, according to *our* conception, should bear some proportion to the offense. Why then eternal punishment for the temporary offenses of so frail a creature as man? . . . Heaven and hell suppose two distinct species of men, the good and the bad; but the greatest part of mankind float betwixt vice and virtue. . . .

The chief source of moral ideas is the reflection on the interests of human society. Ought these interests, so short, so frivolous, to be guarded by punishments eternal and infinite? . . .

Nature has rendered human infancy peculiarly frail and mortal, as it were on purpose to refute the notion of a probationary state; the half of mankind die before they are rational creatures. . . .

Nothing in this world is perpetual; everything, however seemingly firm, is in continual flux and change: The world itself gives symptoms of frailty and dissolution. How contrary to analogy, therefore, to imagine that one single [human] form, seeming the frailest of any, and subject to the greatest disorders, is immortal and indissoluble? What theory is that! How lightly, not to say how rashly, entertained! . . .

How to dispose of the infinite number of [deceased persons] ought also to embarrass the religious theory. Every planet in every solar system, we are at liberty to imagine peopled with intelligent mortal beings, at least we can fix on no other supposition. For these then a new universe must every generation be created . . . to admit of this continual influx of beings. . . .

. . . Death is in the end unavoidable. . . . All doctrines are to be suspected which are favored by our passions; and the hopes and fears which gave rise to this doctrine are very obvious. . . . ("On the Immortality of the Soul")

7. Whence Religion?

. . . As the *causes* which bestow happiness or misery are, in general, very little known and very uncertain, our anxious concern endeavors to attain a determinate idea of them, and finds no better expedient than to represent them as intelligent, voluntary agents, like ourselves; only somewhat superior in power and wisdom. . . . (*The Natural History of Religion*, Section V)

. . . Rather than relinquish this propensity to adulation, religionists in all ages have involved themselves in the greatest absurdities and contradictions. (Ibid., Section VI)

8. Paganism Is in Some Respects Superior to Christian Monotheism

. . . The tolerating spirit of idolaters, both in ancient and modern times, is very obvious to anyone who is the least conversant in the writings of historians or travelers. When the oracle of Delphi was asked, what rites or worship was most acceptable to the Gods? "Those legally established in each city," replied the oracle. . . .

. . . So sociable is polytheism, that the utmost fierceness and aversion which it meets with in an opposite religion is scarcely able to disgust it, and keep it at a distance. Augustus praised extremely the reserve of his grandson, Caius Caesar, when this latter prince, passing by Jerusalem, deigned not to sacrifice according to the Jewish law. But for what reason did Augustus so much approve of this conduct? Only because that religion was by the Pagans esteemed ignoble and barbarous. . . . (Ibid., Section IX)

. . . Where the deity is represented as infinitely superior to mankind, this belief, . . . is apt, when joined with superstitious terrors, to sink the human mind into the lowest submission and abasement, and to represent the monkish virtues of mortification, penance, humility, and passive suffering, as the only qualities which are acceptable to him. . . .

Bellarmine patiently and humbly allowed the fleas and other odious vermin to prey upon him. "We shall have heaven," said he, "to reward us for our sufferings; but these poor creatures have nothing but the enjoyment of the present life." Such difference is there between the maxims of a Greek hero and a Catholic saint. (Ibid., Section X)

9. Christianity, Even More than Other Religions, Should Be Regarded as Absurd

. . . It must be allowed that the Roman Catholics are a very learned sect, and that no one communion but that of the Church of England can dispute their being the

most learned of all the Christian Churches.
Yet Averroes, the famous Arabian, who,
no doubt, has heard of the Egyptian superstitions, declares that of all religions
the most absurd and nonsensical is that
whose votaries eat, after having created,
their deity. . . . (Ibid., Section XII)

10. Religion Also Brings Unintended Consequences

. . . In life . . . good and ill are universally intermingled and confounded; happiness and
misery, wisdom and folly, virtue and vice.
Nothing is purely and entirely of a piece. All
advantages are attended with disadvantages.
. . . The more exquisite any good is, of which
a small specimen is afforded us, the sharper
is the evil allied to it; and few exceptions are
found to this uniform law of nature. . . . As
the good, the great, the sublime, the ravishing, are found eminently in the genuine principles of theism; it may be expected, from the
analogy of nature, that the base, the absurd,
the mean, the terrifying, will be discovered
equally in religious fictions and chimeras. . . .

Survey most nations and most ages. Examine
the religious principles which have, in

fact, prevailed in the world. You will scarcely be persuaded that they are other than sick men's dreams. . . . [There are] no theological absurdities so glaring as have not, sometimes, been embraced by men of the greatest and most cultivated understanding. No religious precepts so rigorous as have not been adopted by the most voluptuous and most abandoned of men. . . . What so pure as some of the morals included in some theological systems? What so corrupt as some of the practices to which these systems give rise?

The comfortable views exhibited by the belief of futurity are ravishing and delightful. But how quickly they vanish on the appearance of its terrors, which keep a more firm and durable possession of the human mind! (Ibid., Section XV)

11. It Is Best to Escape This Realm of "Fury and Contention"

The whole is a riddle, an enigma, an inexplicable mystery. Doubt, uncertainty, suspense of judgment, appear the only result of our most accurate scrutiny concerning this subject. But such is the frailty of human reason, and such the irresistible contagion of opinion, that even this deliberate doubt could scarcely be upheld, did we not enlarge our view, and, opposing one species of superstition to another, set them a quarrelling; while we ourselves, during their fury and contention, happily make our escape into the calm, though obscure, regions of philosophy. (Ibid.)

12. Traditional Philosophical Arguments for the Existence of God Are Flawed

What follows, is taken from the *Dialogues Concerning Natural Religion*, written in 1751, but held back from publication because of its controversial nature until 1779, three years after Hume's death. This work presents a debate between three fictional characters:

- PHILO, a skeptical philosopher who believes conventional religion does more harm than good;

- CLEANTHES, who wants to reconcile Christian faith and reason, who bases his arguments on experience alone, and who rejects logical proofs of God's existence, and;

- DEMEA, a traditional Christian whose religion is based on faith, but who also accepts logical proofs of God's existence.

It is believed that Philo speaks for Hume both in general and in the famous refutations of the philosophical "proofs" for God's existence, the argument from design (the world shows the handiwork of a master designer) and the ontological argument (to be perfect, God must be).

PHILO (skeptic):

"... Let us become thoroughly sensible of the weakness, blindness, and narrow limits of human reason; let us duly consider its uncertainty and endless contrarieties, even in subjects of common life and practice; let the errors and deceits of our very senses be set before us. ...

"... When we look beyond human affairs, ... when we carry our speculations into the two eternities, ... we must be far removed from the smallest tendency to skepticism not to be apprehensive that we have here got quite beyond the reach of our faculties. So long as we confine our speculations to trade, or morals, or politics, or criticism, we make appeals, every moment, to common sense and experience, which strengthen our philosophical conclusions. ... But, in theological reasonings, we have not this advantage. ..." (Part I)

CLEANTHES (Christian reconciler of faith and reason with an emphasis on experience):

"…I shall briefly explain how I conceive this matter. Look round the world, contemplate the whole and every part of it: you will find it to be nothing but one great machine, subdivided into an infinite number of lesser machines, which again admit of subdivisions to a degree beyond what human senses and faculties can trace and explain. All these various machines, and even their most minute parts, are adjusted to each other with an accuracy which ravishes into admiration all men who have ever contemplated them. The curious adapting of means to ends, throughout all nature, resembles exactly, though it much exceeds, the productions of human contrivance; of human designs, thought, wisdom, and intelligence. Since, therefore, the effects resemble each other, we are led to infer, by all the rules of analogy, that the causes also resemble; and that the Author of Nature is somewhat similar to the mind of man. … By this argument *a posteriori*, and by this argument alone, do we prove at once the existence of a Deity, and his similarity to human mind and intelligence."

DEMEA (Christian with emphasis on faith but also on logic):

"I . . . [do] not approve of your conclusion concerning the similarity of the Deity to men; still less can I approve of the mediums by which you endeavor to establish it. What! No demonstration of the Being of God! No abstract arguments! No proofs *a priori*! Are these, which have hitherto been so much insisted on by philosophers, all fallacy, all sophism? Can we reach no further in this subject than experience and probability? I will not say that this is betraying the cause of a Deity: but surely . . . you give advantages to Atheists. . . ."

PHILO (skeptic):

"What I chiefly scruple in this subject," said Philo, "is not so much that all religious arguments are by Cleanthes reduced to experience, as that they appear not to be even the most certain and irrefragable of that inferior kind. That a stone will fall, that fire will burn, that the earth has solidity, we have observed a thousand and a thousand times; and when any new instance of this nature is presented, we draw without hesitation the accustomed inference. The exact similarity of the cases gives us a perfect assurance of a similar event; and a stronger evidence is never desired nor sought after. But wherever you depart, in the least, from the similarity of the cases, you diminish proportionally the evidence; and may at last bring it to a very weak analogy, which is confessedly liable to error and uncertainty. . . .

"If we see a house, Cleanthes, we conclude, with the greatest certainty, that it had an architect or builder because this is precisely that species of effect which we have experienced to proceed from that species of cause. But surely you will not affirm that the universe bears such a resemblance to a house that we can with the same certainty infer a similar cause, or that the analogy is here entire and perfect. The dissimilitude is so striking that the utmost you can here pretend to is a guess. . . .

"But allowing that we were to take the operations of one part of nature upon another for the foundation of our judgment concerning the origin of the whole (which never can be admitted), yet why select so minute, so weak, so bounded a principle as the reason and design of animals is found to be upon this planet? What peculiar privilege has this little agitation of the brain which we call thought, that we must thus make it the model of the whole universe? Our partiality in our own favor does indeed present it on all occasions, but sound philosophy ought carefully to guard against so natural an illusion. . . .

"And can you blame me, Cleanthes, if I here imitate the prudent reserve of Simonides, who, according to the noted story, being asked by Hiero, *What God was*? desired a day to think of it, and then two days more; and after that manner continually prolonged the term, without ever bringing in his definition or description? Could you even blame me if I had answered, at first, that I did not know, and was sensible that this subject lay vastly beyond the reach of my faculties? You might cry out skeptic . . . as much as you pleased: but, having found in so many other subjects much more familiar the imperfections and even contradictions of human reason, I never should expect any success from its feeble conjectures in a subject so sublime and so remote from the sphere of our observation. . . ." (Part II)

DEMEA (Christian with emphasis on faith but also on logic):

"... In reality, Cleanthes, consider what it is you assert, when you represent the deity as similar to a human mind and understanding.... New opinions, new passions, new affections, new feelings arise, which continually diversify the ... [human] mental scene, and produce in it the greatest variety, and most rapid succession imaginable. How is this compatible, with that perfect immutability and simplicity, which all true theists ascribe to the deity?"

PHILO (skeptic):

[Also addressing Cleanthes: "And]...how... shall we satisfy ourselves concerning the cause of that Being whom you suppose the Author of nature, or, according to your system of anthropomorphism, the ideal world.... If the material world rests upon a similar ideal world, this ideal world must rest upon some other, and so on without end. It were better, therefore, never to look beyond the present material world.... (Part IV)

"And why not become a perfect anthropomorphite? Why not assert the deity or deities to be corporeal, and to have eyes, a nose, mouth, ears, etc.? Epicurus maintained that no man had ever seen reason but in a human figure; therefore, the gods must have a human figure. And this argument, which is deservedly so much ridiculed by Cicero, becomes, according to you, solid and philosophical.

"In a word, Cleanthes, a man who follows your hypothesis is able, perhaps, to assert or conjecture that the universe sometime arose from something like design; but beyond that position he cannot ascertain one single circumstance, and is left afterwards to fix every point of his theology by the utmost license of fancy and hypothesis. This world, for aught he knows, is very faulty and imperfect, compared to a superior standard, and was only the first rude essay of some infant deity who afterwards abandoned it, ashamed of his lame performance; it is the work only of some dependent, inferior deity, and is the object of derision to his superiors; it is the production of old age and dotage in some superannuated deity, and ever since his death has run on at adventures, from the first impulse and active force which it received from him. You justly give signs of horror, Demea, at these strange suppositions; but these, and a thousand more of the same kind, are Cleanthes's suppositions, not mine. From the moment the attributes of the Deity are supposed finite, all these have place. And I cannot, for my part, think that so wild and unsettled a system of theology is, in any respect, preferable to none at all. . . ." (Part V)

. . . Philo continued. . . . "A tree bestows order and organization on that tree which springs from it . . . ; an animal in the same manner on its offspring; a bird on its nest; and instances of this kind are even more frequent in the world than those of order which arise from reason and contrivance. . . . Why an orderly system may not be spun from the belly as well as from the brain, it will be difficult for . . . Cleanthes to give a satisfactory reason. . . . (Part VII)

["But let us set this abstract argument aside for a moment"] . . . , said Philo, ["and consider] the curious artifices of nature, . . . [that] embitter the life of every living being. The stronger prey upon the weaker, and keep them in perpetual terror and anxiety. The weaker too, in their turn, often prey upon the stronger. . . . On each hand, before and behind, above and below, every animal is surrounded with enemies, which incessantly seek his misery and destruction. . . .

"Man, it is true, can, by combination, surmount all his real enemies, and become master of the whole animal creation; but does he not immediately raise up to himself imaginary enemies, the demons of his fancy, who haunt him with superstitious terrors, and blast every enjoyment of life? His pleasure, as he imagines, becomes in their eyes a crime; his food and repose give them umbrage and offense; his very sleep and dreams furnish new materials to anxious fear; and even death, his refuge from every other ill, presents only the dread of endless and innumerable woes. . . .

"Besides, . . . this very society, by which we surmount those wild beasts, our natural enemies, what new enemies does it not raise to us? What woe and misery does it not occasion? Man is the greatest enemy of man. Oppression, injustice, contempt, contumely, violence, sedition, war, calumny, treachery, fraud—by these they mutually torment each other, and they would soon dissolve that society which they had formed, were it not for the dread of still greater ills, which must attend their separation. . . .

"Is it possible, Cleanthes," said Philo, "that after all these reflections, and infinitely more, which might be suggested, you can still persevere in your anthropomorphism, and assert the moral attributes of the Deity, his justice, benevolence, mercy, and rectitude, to be of the same nature with these virtues in human creatures? His power, we allow, is infinite; whatever he wills is executed; but neither man nor any other animal is happy; therefore, he does not will their happiness. His wisdom is infinite; He is never mistaken in choosing the means to any end; but the course of nature tends not to human or animal felicity; therefore it is not established for that purpose. Through the whole compass of human knowledge, there are no inferences more certain and infallible than these. In what respect, then, do his benevolence and mercy resemble the benevolence and mercy of men?

"Epicurus's old questions are yet unanswered. Is he willing to prevent evil, but not able? Then is he impotent. Is he able, but not willing? Then is he malevolent. Is he both able and willing? Whence then is evil?...

"This is not, by any means, what we expect from infinite power, infinite wisdom, and infinite goodness. Why is there any misery at all in the world?... (Part X) There may be four hypotheses ... framed concerning the first causes of the universe: that they are endowed with perfect goodness; that they have perfect malice; that they are opposite, and have both goodness and malice; that they have neither goodness nor malice. Mixed phenomena can never prove the two former unmixed principles; and the uniformity and steadiness of general laws seem to oppose the third. The fourth, therefore, seems by far the most probable...." (Part XI)

DEMEA (Christian with emphasis on faith, but also on logic):

"... If so many difficulties attend the argument *a posteriori*," said Demea, "had we not better adhere to that simple and sublime argument *a priori* which, by offering to us infallible demonstration, cuts off at once all doubt and difficulty?... For how can an effect, which either is finite, or, for aught we know, may be so—how can such an effect, I say, prove an infinite cause? The unity, too, of the Divine Nature, it is very difficult, if not absolutely impossible, to deduce merely from contemplating the works of nature. . . .

"The [*a priori*] argument . . . which I would insist on, is . . . [as follows]. Whatever exists must have a cause or reason of its existence; it being absolutely impossible for anything to produce itself, or be the cause of its own existence. In mounting up, therefore, from effects to causes, we must either go on in tracing an infinite succession, without any ultimate cause at all; or must at last have recourse to some ultimate cause, that is necessarily existent. Now, . . . the first supposition is absurd. . . . The question . . . still . . . [remains] why this particular succession of causes existed from eternity, and not any other succession, or no succession at all. . . .We must, therefore, have recourse to a necessarily existent Being, who carries the reason of his existence in himself, and who cannot be supposed not to exist, without an express contradiction. There is, consequently, such a Being; that is, there is a deity."

Cleanthes (Christian reconciler of faith and reason, with emphasis on experience):

"I shall not leave it to Philo," said Cleanthes, "to point out the weakness of . . . [Demea's endorsement of a purely logical proof, unrelated to experience, for the existence of God]. It seems to me so obviously ill-grounded, and at the same time of so little consequence to the cause of true piety and religion, that I shall myself venture to show the fallacy of it.

"I shall begin with observing, that there is an evident absurdity in pretending to demonstrate a matter of fact, or to prove it by any arguments *a priori*. Nothing is demonstrable unless the contrary implies a contradiction. . . . [But] . . . whatever we conceive as existent, we can also conceive as non-existent. There is no being, therefore, whose non-existence implies a contradiction. Consequently there is no being, whose existence is demonstrable. I propose this argument as entirely decisive, and am willing to rest the whole controversy upon it.

"It is pretended that the Deity is a necessarily existent being; and this necessity of his existence is attempted to be explained by asserting, that if we knew his whole essence or nature, we should perceive it to be as impossible for him not to exist, as for twice two not to be four. But it is evident that this can never happen, while our faculties remain the same as at present. It will still be possible for us, at any time, to conceive the non-existence of what we formerly conceived to exist. . . . The words, therefore, necessary existence, have no meaning; or, which is the same thing; none that is consistent. . . ."

Philo (skeptic):

"Though the reasonings which you have urged, Cleanthes, may well excuse me," said Philo, "from starting any further difficulties, yet I cannot forbear insisting still upon another . . . [argument]. It is observed by arithmeticians, that the products of 9, compose always either 9, or some . . . product of 9, if you add together all the characters of which any of the former products is composed. Thus, of 18, 27, 36, which are products of 9, you make 9 by adding 1 to 8, 2 to 7, 3 to 6. Thus, 369 is a product also of 9; and if you add 3, 6, and 9, you make 18, a . . . product of 9. To a superficial observer, so wonderful a regularity may be admired as the effect either of chance or design; but a skillful algebraist immediately concludes it to be the work of necessity, and demonstrates, that it must forever result from the nature of these numbers. Is it not probable, I ask, that the whole economy of the universe is conducted by a like necessity, though no human algebra can furnish a key which solves the difficulty? And instead of admiring the order of natural beings, may it not happen, that, could we penetrate into the intimate nature of bodies, we should clearly see why it was absolutely impossible they could ever admit of any other disposition? So dangerous is it to introduce this idea of necessity into the present question! And so naturally does it afford an inference directly opposite to the religious hypothesis! . . . (Part IX)

"[But there is only so far we can go in this way.] . . . All men of sound reason are disgusted with verbal disputes, which abound so much in philosophical and theological inquiries; and it is found, that the only remedy for this abuse must arise from clear definitions, from the precision of those ideas which enter into any argument, and from the strict and uniform use of those terms which are employed. But there is a species of controversy, which, from the very nature of language and of human ideas, is involved in perpetual ambiguity, and can never, by any precaution or any definitions, be able to reach a reasonable certainty or precision. These are the controversies concerning the degrees of any quality or circumstance. Men may argue to all eternity, whether Hannibal be a great, or a very great, or a superlatively great man, what degree of beauty Cleopatra possessed. . . . That the dispute concerning theism is of this nature, and consequently is merely verbal, or perhaps, if possible, still more incurably ambiguous, will appear upon the slightest inquiry. . . .

". . . This is well understood in the world; and none but fools ever repose less trust in a man, because they hear, that from study and philosophy, he has entertained some speculative doubts with regard to theological subjects. And when we have to do with a man, who makes a great profession of religion and devotion, has this any other effect upon several, who pass for prudent, than to put them on their guard, lest they be cheated and deceived by him? . . .

"... It is contrary to common sense to entertain apprehensions or terrors upon account of any opinion whatsoever, or to imagine that we run any risk hereafter, by the freest use of our reason. Such a sentiment implies both an absurdity and an inconsistency. It is an absurdity to believe that the Deity has human passions, and one of the lowest of human passions, a restless appetite for applause. It is an inconsistency to believe, that, since the Deity has this human passion, he has not others also, and, in particular, a disregard to the opinions of creatures so much inferior." (Part XII)

—HUNTER LEWIS

An Enquiry Concerning Human Understanding

(1748)

Section I, 6

A CONSIDERABLE PART OF [philosophy or theology] . . . arise[s] either from the fruitless efforts of human vanity, which would penetrate into subjects utterly inaccessible to the understanding, or from the craft of popular superstitions which, being unable to defend themselves on fair ground, raise these entangling brambles to cover and protect their weakness. Chased from the open country, these robbers fly into the forest, and lie in wait to break in upon every unguarded avenue of the mind, and overwhelm it with religious fears and prejudices. . . .

Section X: Of Miracles

Part I

Nothing is so convenient as a decisive argument . . . , which must . . . *silence* the most arrogant bigotry and superstition, and free us from their impertinent solicitations. I flatter myself, that I have discovered an argument . . . , which, if just, will, with the wise and learned, be an everlasting check to all kinds of superstitious delusion, and consequently, will be useful as long as the world endures. For so long, I presume, will the accounts of miracles and prodigies be found in all history, sacred and profane. . . .

A wise man . . . proportions his belief to the evidence. In such conclusions as are founded on an infallible experience, he expects the event with the last degree of assurance, and regards his past experience as a full *proof* of the future existence of that event. In other cases, he proceeds with more caution: He weighs the opposite experiments. He considers which side is supported by the greater number of experiments; to that side he inclines, with doubt and hesitation. And when at last he fixes his judgment, the evidence exceeds not what we properly call *probability*. All probability, then, supposes an opposition of experiments and observations, where the one side is found to overbalance the other, and to produce a degree of evidence, proportioned to the superiority. A hundred instances or experiments on one side, and fifty on another, afford a doubtful expectation of any event; though a hundred uniform experiments, with only one that is contradictory, reasonably beget a pretty strong degree of assurance. In all cases, we must balance the opposite experiments, where they are opposite, and deduct the smaller number from the greater, in order to know the exact force of the superior evidence.

To apply these principles to a particular instance; we may observe, that there is no species of reasoning more common, more useful, and even necessary to human life, than that which is derived from the testimony of men, and the reports of eye-witnesses and spectators.... As the evidence, derived from witnesses and human testimony, is founded on past experience, so it varies with the experience, and is regarded either as a *proof* or a *probability*.... There are a number of circumstances to be taken into consideration in all judgments of this kind; and the ultimate standard, by which we determine all disputes, that may arise concerning them, is always derived from experience and observation....

We entertain a suspicion concerning any matter of fact, when the witnesses contradict each other; when they are but few, or of a doubtful character; when they have an interest in what they affirm; when they deliver their testimony with hesitation, or on the contrary, with too violent asseverations ..., [or when] ... the testimony ... partakes of the extraordinary and the marvelous.... *I should not believe such a story were it told me by Cato*, was a proverbial saying in Rome, even during the lifetime of that philosophical patriot. The incredibility of a fact, it was allowed, might invalidate so great an authority.... But in order to increase the probability against the testimony of witnesses, let us suppose, that the fact, which they affirm, instead of being only marvelous, is really miraculous....

A miracle is a violation of the laws of nature; ... There must ... be a uniform experience against every miraculous event, otherwise the event would not merit that appellation. And as a uniform experience amounts to a proof, there is here a direct and full *proof*, from the nature of the fact, against the existence of any miracle; nor can such a proof be destroyed, or the miracle rendered credible, but by an opposite proof, which is superior.

The plain consequence is (and it is a general maxim worthy of our attention) that no testimony is sufficient to establish a miracle, unless the testimony be of such a kind, that its falsehood would be more miraculous, than the fact, which it endeavors to establish; and even in that case there is a mutual destruction of arguments, and the superior only gives us an assurance suitable to that degree of force, which remains, after deducting the inferior. When anyone tells me, that he saw a dead man restored to life, I immediately consider with myself, whether it be more probable, that this person should either deceive or be deceived, or that the fact, which he relates, should really have happened. I weigh the one miracle against the other; and according to the superiority, which I discover, I pronounce my decision, and always reject the greater miracle. If the falsehood of his testimony would be more miraculous, than the event which he relates; then, and not till then, can he pretend to command my belief or opinion.

Part II

It is easy to show, that we have been a great deal too liberal in our concession, and that there never was a miraculous event established on so full an evidence.

For *first*, there is not to be found, in all history, any miracle attested by a sufficient number of men, of such unquestioned good-sense, education, and learning, as to secure us against all delusion in themselves; of such undoubted integrity, as to place them beyond all suspicion of any design to deceive others; of such credit and reputation in the eyes of mankind, as to have a great deal to lose in case of their being detected in any falsehood; and at the same time, attesting facts performed in such a public manner and in so celebrated a part of the world, as to render the detection unavoidable: All which circumstances are requisite to give us a full assurance in the testimony of men.

Secondly. We may observe in human nature a principle which, if strictly examined, will be found to diminish extremely the assurance, which we might, from human testimony, have, in any kind of prodigy. The maxim, by which we commonly conduct ourselves in our reasonings, is, that the objects, of which we have no experience, resemble those, of which we have; that what we have found to be most usual is always most probable; and that where there is an opposition of arguments, we ought to give the preference to such as are founded on the greatest number of past observations. But though, in proceeding by this rule, we readily reject any fact which is unusual and incredible in an ordinary degree; yet in advancing farther, the mind observes not always the same rule; but when anything is affirmed utterly absurd and miraculous, it rather the more readily admits of such a fact, upon account of that very circumstance, which ought to destroy all its authority. . . .

The many instances of forged miracles, and prophecies, and supernatural events, which, in all ages, have either been detected by contrary evidence, or which detect themselves by their absurdity, prove sufficiently the strong propensity of mankind to the extraordinary and the marvelous, and ought reasonably to beget a suspicion against all relations of this kind. . . .

Thirdly. It forms a strong presumption against all supernatural and miraculous relations, that they are observed chiefly to abound among ignorant and barbarous nations; or if a civilized people has ever given admission to any of them, that people will be found to have received them from ignorant and barbarous ancestors, who transmitted them with that inviolable sanction and authority, which always attends received opinions. . . .

It is strange, a judicious reader is apt to say, upon the perusal of these wonderful historians, *that such prodigious events never happen in our days*. But it is nothing strange, I hope, that men should lie in all ages. You must surely have seen instances enough of that frailty. You have yourself heard many such marvelous relations started, which, being treated with scorn by all the wise and judicious, have at last been abandoned even by the vulgar. Be assured, that those renowned lies, which have spread and flourished to such a monstrous height, arose from like beginnings; but being sown in a more proper soil, shot up at last into prodigies almost equal to those which they relate. . . .

I may add as a *fourth* reason, which diminishes the authority of prodigies, that . . . whatever is different is contrary; . . . all the prodigies of different religions are to be regarded as contrary facts, and the evidences of these prodigies, whether weak or strong, as opposite to each other. . . . This argument may appear over subtle and refined; but is not in reality different from the reasoning of a judge, who supposes, that the credit of two witnesses, maintaining a crime against any one, is destroyed by the testimony of two others. . . . The contrariety is equally strong between the miracles related by Herodotus or Plutarch, and those delivered by Mariana, Bede, or any monkish historian. . . .

How many stories of this nature have, in all ages, been detected and exploded in their infancy? How many more have been celebrated for a time, and have afterwards sunk into neglect and oblivion? Where such reports, therefore, fly about, the solution of the phenomenon is obvious; and we judge in conformity to regular experience and observation, when we account for it by the known and natural principles of credulity and delusion. And shall we, rather than have a recourse to so natural a solution, allow of a miraculous violation of the most established laws of nature? . . .

In the infancy of new religions, the wise and learned commonly esteem the matter too inconsiderable to deserve their attention or regard. And when afterwards they would willingly detect the cheat, in order to undeceive the deluded multitude, the season is now past, and the records and witnesses, which might clear up the matter, have perished beyond recovery. . . .

Upon the whole, then, it appears, that no testimony for any kind of miracle has ever amounted to a probability, much less to a proof; and that, even supposing it amounted to a proof, it would be opposed by another proof; derived from the very nature of the fact, which it would endeavor to establish. It is experience only, which gives authority to human testimony; and it is the same experience, which assures us of the laws of nature. When, therefore, these two kinds of experience are contrary, we have nothing to do but subtract the one from the other, and embrace an opinion, either on one side or the other, with that assurance which arises from the remainder. But according to the principle here explained, this subtraction, with regard to all popular religions, amounts to an entire annihilation; and therefore we may establish it as a maxim, that no human testimony can have such force as to prove a miracle, and make it a just foundation for any such system of religion. . . .

Lord Bacon seems to have embraced the same principles of reasoning. "We ought," says he, "to make a collection or particular history of all monsters and prodigious births or productions, and in a word of everything new, rare, and extraordinary in nature. But this must be done with the most severe scrutiny, lest we depart from truth. Above all, every relation must be considered as suspicious, which depends in any degree upon religion, as the prodigies of Livy. And no less so, everything that is to be found in the writers of natural magic or alchemy, or such authors, who seem, all of them, to have an unconquerable appetite for falsehood and fable. . . ."

. . . Let us [also] examine those miracles, related in scripture; and not to lose ourselves in too wide a field, . . . confine ourselves to such as we find in the Pentateuch. . . . Here . . . we . . . consider a book, presented to us by a barbarous and ignorant people, written in an age when they were still more barbarous, and in all probability long after the facts which it relates, corroborated by no concurring testimony, and resembling those fabulous accounts, which every nation gives of its origin. Upon reading this book, we find it full of prodigies and miracles. It gives an account of a state of the world and of human nature entirely different from the present: of our fall from that state; of the age of man, extended to near a thousand years; of the destruction of the world by a deluge; of the arbitrary choice of one people, as the favorites of heaven; and that people the countrymen of the author; of their deliverance from bondage by prodigies the most astonishing imaginable. I desire any one to lay his hand upon his heart, and after a serious consideration declare, whether he thinks that the falsehood of such a book, supported by such a testimony, would be more extraordinary and miraculous than all the miracles it relates; which is, however, necessary to make it be received, according to the measures of probability above established.

What we have said of miracles may be applied, without any variation, to prophecies; and indeed, all prophecies are real miracles, and as such only, can be admitted as proofs of any revelation. If it did not exceed the capacity of human nature to foretell future events, it would be absurd to employ any prophecy as an argument for a divine mission or authority from heaven. So that, upon the whole, we may conclude, that the *Christian Religion* not only was at first attended with miracles, but even at this day cannot be believed by any reasonable person without one. Mere reason is insufficient to convince us of its veracity: And whoever is moved by *Faith* to assent to it, is conscious of a continued miracle in his own person, which subverts all the principles of his understanding, and gives him a determination to believe what is most contrary to custom and experience.

An Enquiry Concerning the Principles of Morals

(1751)

Section IX: Conclusion

Part I

CELIBACY, FASTING, PENANCE, mortification, self-denial, humility, silence, solitude,
and the whole train of monkish virtues; for
what reason are they everywhere rejected by men of
sense, but because they serve to no manner of purpose; neither advance a man's fortune in the world,
nor render him a more valuable member of society;
neither qualify him for the entertainment of company, nor increase his power of self-enjoyment? We

observe, on the contrary, that they cross all these desirable ends; stupefy the understanding and harden the heart, obscure the fancy and sour the temper. We justly, therefore, transfer them to the opposite column, and place them in the catalog of vices; nor has any superstition force sufficient among men of the world, to pervert entirely these natural sentiments. A gloomy, hairbrained enthusiast, after his death, may have a place in the calendar; but will scarcely ever be admitted, when alive, into intimacy and society, except by those who are as delirious and dismal as himself.

Selected Essays

(1742)

Of Suicide

ONE CONSIDERABLE ADVANTAGE, that arises from philosophy, consists in the sovereign antidote, which it affords to superstition and false religion. All other remedies against that pestilent distemper are vain, or, at least, uncertain. Plain good-sense, and the practice of the world, which alone serve most purposes of life, are here found ineffectual: History, as well as daily experience, affords instances of men, endowed with the strongest capacity for business and affairs, who have all their lives crouched under slavery to the grossest superstition. Even gaiety and sweetness of temper, which infuse a balm into every other wound, afford no remedy to so virulent a poison. . . . But when sound philosophy has once gained possession of the mind, superstition is effectually excluded; and one may safely affirm, that her triumph over this enemy is more complete than over most of the vices and imperfections, incident to human nature. Love or anger, ambition or avarice, have their root in the temper and affections, which the soundest reason is scarce ever able fully to correct. But superstition, being founded on false opinion, must immediately vanish, when true philosophy has inspired juster sentiments of superior powers. . . .

It will here be superfluous to magnify the merits of philosophy, by displaying the pernicious tendency of that vice, of which it cures the human mind. The superstitious man, says Tully [Cicero], is miserable in every scene, in every incident of life. Even sleep itself, which banishes all other cares of unhappy mortals, affords to him matter of new terror; while he examines his dreams, and finds in those visions of the night, prognostications of future calamities.

Of Superstition and Enthusiasm

These two species of false religion, though both pernicious, are yet of a very different, and even of a contrary nature. The mind of man is subject to certain unaccountable terrors and apprehensions, proceeding either from the unhappy situation of private or public affairs, from ill health, from a gloomy and melancholy disposition, or from the concurrence of all these circumstances. In such a state of mind, infinite unknown evils are dreaded from unknown agents; and where real objects of terror are wanting, the soul, active to its own prejudice, and fostering its predominant inclination, finds imaginary ones, to whose power and malevolence it sets no limits. As these enemies are entirely invisible and unknown, the methods taken to appease them are equally unaccountable, and consist in ceremonies, observances, mortifications, sacrifices, presents, or in any practice, however absurd or frivolous, which either folly or knavery recommends to a blind and terrified credulity. Weakness, fear, melancholy, together with ignorance, are, therefore, the true sources of superstition.

But the mind of man is also subject to an unaccountable elevation and presumption, arising from prosperous success, from luxuriant health, from strong spirits, or from a bold and confident disposition. In such a state of mind, the imagination swells with great, but confused conceptions, to which no sublunary beauties or enjoyments can correspond. Everything mortal and perishable vanishes as unworthy of attention; and a full range is given to the fancy in the invisible regions, or world of Spirits, where the soul is at liberty to indulge itself in every imagination, which may best suit its present taste and disposition. Hence arise raptures, transports, and surprising flights of fancy; and, confidence and presumption still increasing, these raptures, being altogether unaccountable, and seeming quite beyond the reach of our ordinary faculties, are attributed to the immediate inspiration of that Divine Being who is the object of devotion. In a little time, the inspired person comes to regard himself as a distinguished favorite of the Divinity; and when this frenzy once takes place, which is the summit of enthusiasm, every whimsy is consecrated; human reason, and even morality, are rejected as fallacious guides; and the fanatic madman delivers himself over, blindly and without reserve, to the . . . Spirit, and to inspiration from above. Hope, pride, presumption, a warm imagination, together with ignorance, are therefore the true sources of enthusiasm. . . .

. . . *Religions which partake of enthusiasm, are, on their first rise, more furious and violent than those which partake of superstition; but in a little time become more gentle and moderate.* The violence of this species of religion, when excited by novelty, and animated by opposition, appears from numberless instances; of the *Anabaptists* in Germany, the *Camisars* in France, the *Levelers,* and other fanatics in England, and the *Covenanters* in Scotland. Enthusiasm being founded on strong spirits, and a presumptuous boldness of character, it naturally begets the most extreme resolutions;

especially after it rises to that height as to inspire the deluded fanatic with the opinion of Divine illuminations, and with a contempt for the common rules of reason, morality, and prudence.

It is thus enthusiasm produces the most cruel disorders in human society; but its fury is like that of thunder and tempest, which exhaust themselves in a little time, and leave the air more calm and serene than before. When the first fire of enthusiasm is spent, men naturally, in all fanatical sects, sink into the greatest remissness and coolness in sacred matters; there being no body of men among them endowed with sufficient authority, whose interest is concerned to support the religious spirit; no rites, no ceremonies, no holy observances, which may enter into the common train of life, and preserve the sacred principles from oblivion. Superstition, on the contrary, steals in gradually and insensibly; renders men tame and submissive; is acceptable to the magistrate, and seems inoffensive to the people; till at last the priest, having firmly established his authority, becomes the tyrant and disturber of human society, by his endless contentions, persecutions, and religious wars. How smoothly did the Romish church advance in her acquisition of power? But into what dismal convulsions did she throw all Europe, in order to maintain it? On the other hand, our sectaries, who were formerly such dangerous bigots, are now become very free reasoners; and the *Quakers* seem to approach nearly the only regular body of *deists* in the universe, the *literati,* or the disciples of Confucius in China.

My *third* observation on this head is, *that superstition is an enemy to civil liberty, and enthusiasm a friend to it.* As superstition groans under the dominion of priests, and enthusiasm is destructive of all ecclesiastical power, this sufficiently accounts for the present observation. Not to mention that enthusiasm, being the infirmity of bold and ambitious tempers, is naturally accompanied with a spirit of liberty; as superstition, on the contrary, renders men tame and abject, and fits them for slavery. We learn from English history, that, during the civil wars, the *independents* and *deists,* though the most opposite in their religious principles, yet were united in their political ones, and were alike passionate for a commonwealth. And since the origin of *Whig* and *Tory,* the leaders of the *Whigs* have either been *deists* or professed *latitudinarians* in their principles; that is, friends to toleration, and indifferent to any particular sect of *Christians*: While the sectaries, who have all a strong tincture of enthusiasm, have always, without exception, concurred with that party in defense of civil liberty. The resemblance in their superstitions long united the High-Church *Tories* and the *Roman Catholics*, in support of prerogative and kingly power. . . .

The *Molinists* and *Jansenists* in France have a thousand unintelligible disputes, which are not worthy the reflection of a man of sense: but what principally distinguishes these two sects, and alone merits attention, is the different spirit of their religion. The *Molinists,* conducted by the *Jesuits,* are great friends to superstition, rigid observers of external forms and ceremonies, and devoted to the authority of the priests, and to tradition. The *Jansenists* are enthusiasts, and zealous promoters of the passionate devotion, and of the inward life; little influenced by authority; and, in a word, but half Catholics. The consequences are exactly conformable to the foregoing reasoning. The *Jesuits* are the tyrants of the people, and the slaves of the court: and the *Jansenists* preserve alive the small sparks of the love of liberty which are to be found in the French nation.

Of National Characters

It is a trite, but not altogether a false maxim, that *priests of all religions are the same.* . . . These men, being elevated above humanity, acquire a uniform character, which is entirely their own, and which, in my opinion, is, generally speaking, not the most amiable that is to be met with in human society. . . .

The human mind is of a very imitative nature; nor is it possible for any set of men to converse often together, without acquiring a similitude of manner, and communicating to each other their vices as well as virtues. The propensity to company and society is strong in all rational creatures; and the same disposition, which gives us this propensity, makes us enter deeply into each other's sentiments, and causes like passions and inclinations to run, as it were, by contagion, through the whole club or knot of companions. . . .

Of the Parties of Great Britain

We may observe, that, in all ages of the world, priests have been enemies to liberty; and, it is certain, that this steady conduct of theirs must have been founded on fixed reasons of interest and ambition. Liberty of thinking, and of expressing our thoughts, is always fatal to priestly power, and to those pious frauds on which it is commonly founded. . . .

On the Standard of Taste

The same good sense that directs men in the ordinary occurrences of life, is not hearkened to in religious matters, which are supposed to be placed altogether above the cognizance of human reason. . . . No religious principles can ever be imputed as a fault to any poet, while they remain merely principles, and take not such strong possession of his heart as to lay him under the imputation of *bigotry* or *superstition*. . . .

Religious principles are also a blemish in any polite composition, when they . . . intrude themselves into every sentiment, however remote from any connection with religion. . . . It must forever be ridiculous in Petrarch to compare his mistress, Laura, to Jesus Christ. Nor is it less ridiculous in that agreeable libertine, Boccace, very seriously to give thanks to God Almighty and the ladies, for their assistance in defending him against his enemies.

On the Immortality of the Soul

Matter . . . and spirit are at bottom equally unknown; and we cannot determine what qualities are inherent in the one or in the other. . . . We cannot know . . . whether matter . . . may not be the cause of thought. . . .

There arise indeed in some minds some unaccountable terrors with regard to futurity; but these would quickly vanish were they not artificially fostered by precept and education. And those who foster them, what is their motive? Only to gain a livelihood, and to acquire power and riches in this world. Their very zeal and industry, therefore, are an argument against them.

What cruelty, what iniquity, what injustice in nature, to confine all our concern, as well as all our knowledge, to the present life, if there be another scene still waiting us of infinitely greater consequence? Ought this barbarous deceit to be ascribed to a beneficent and wise being? . . .

As every effect implies a cause, and that another, till we reach the first cause of all, which is the *Deity*; everything that happens is ordained by him, and nothing can be the object of his punishment or vengeance. . . .

Punishment, according to *our* conception, should bear some proportion to the offense. Why then eternal punishment for the temporary offenses of so frail a creature as man? . . . Heaven and hell suppose two distinct species of men, the good and the bad; but the greatest part of mankind float betwixt vice and virtue. . . .

The chief source of moral ideas is the reflection on the interests of human society. Ought these interests, so short, so frivolous, to be guarded by punishments eternal and infinite? . . .

Nature has rendered human infancy peculiarly frail and mortal, as it were on purpose to refute the notion of a probationary state; the half of mankind die before they are rational creatures. . . .

The souls of animals are allowed to be mortal; and these bear so near a resemblance to the souls of men, that the analogy from one to the other forms a very strong argument. . . .

Nothing in this world is perpetual; everything, however seemingly firm, is in continual flux and change: The world itself gives symptoms of frailty and dissolution; How contrary to analogy, therefore, to imagine that one single [human] form, seeming the frailest of any, and subject to the greatest disorders, is immortal and indissoluble? What theory is that! How lightly, not to say how rashly, entertained! . . .

How to dispose of the infinite number of [deceased persons] ought also to embarrass the religious theory. Every planet in every solar system, we are at liberty to imagine peopled with intelligent mortal beings, at least we can fix on no other supposition. For these then a new universe must every generation be created . . . to admit of this continual influx of beings. . . .

When it is asked, whether *Agamemnon, Thersites, Hannibal, Nero*, and every stupid clown that ever existed in *Italy, Scythia, Bactria*, or *Guinea*, are now alive; can any man think, that a scrutiny of nature will furnish arguments strong enough to answer so strange a question in the affirmative. . . .

. . . Death is in the end unavoidable. . . . All doctrines are to be suspected which are favored by our passions; and the hopes and fears which gave rise to this doctrine are very obvious. . . .

. . . By what arguments or analogies can we prove any state of existence, which no one ever saw, and which no way resembles any that ever was seen? Who will repose such trust in any pretended philosophy as to admit upon its testimony the reality of so marvelous a scene? . . .

The Natural History of Religion

(1757)

Section II

THE FIRST IDEAS of religion arose . . . from the incessant hopes and fears which actuate the human mind: . . . the anxious concern for happiness, the dread of future misery, the terror of death, the thirst of revenge, the appetite for food and other necessaries. Agitated by hopes and fears of this nature, especially the latter, men scrutinize . . . the various and contrary events of human life. And in this disordered scene, with eyes still more disordered and astonished, they see the first obscure traces of divinity.

Section III

... There is a universal tendency amongst mankind to conceive all beings like themselves, and to transfer to every object those qualities with which they are familiarly acquainted, and of which they are intimately conscious. We find human faces in the moon, armies in the clouds; and by a natural propensity, if not corrected by experience and reflection, ascribe malice and good will to everything that hurts or pleases us. ... No wonder, then, that mankind, being placed in such an absolute ignorance of causes, and being at the same time so anxious concerning their future fortunes, should immediately acknowledge a dependence on invisible powers possessed of sentiment and intelligence. ... Nor is it long before we ascribe to them thought, and reason, and passion, and sometimes even the limbs and figures of men, in order to bring them nearer to a resemblance with ourselves. ...

Section V

... As the *causes* which bestow happiness or misery are, in general, very little known and very uncertain, our anxious concern endeavors to attain a determinate idea of them, and finds no better expedient than to represent them as intelligent, voluntary agents, like ourselves; only somewhat superior in power and wisdom. . . . The same principles naturally deify mortals, superior in power, courage, or understanding, and produce hero-worship, together with fabulous history and mythological tradition, in all its wild and unaccountable forms. . . .

Section VI

. . . Rather than relinquish this propensity to adulation, religionists in all ages have involved themselves in the greatest absurdities and contradictions.

Homer, in one passage, calls Oceanus and Tethys the original parents of all things, conformably to the established mythology and traditions of the Greeks. Yet, in other passages, he could not forbear complimenting Jupiter, the reigning deity, with that magnificent appellation; and accordingly denominates him the father of Gods and men. He forgets that every temple, every street, was full of the ancestors, uncles, brothers, and sisters of this Jupiter, who was, in reality, nothing but an upstart parricide and usurper. . . .

Section IX

. . . The tolerating spirit of idolaters, both in ancient and modern times, is very obvious to anyone who is the least conversant in the writings of historians or travelers. When the oracle of Delphi was asked, what rites or worship was most acceptable to the Gods? "Those legally established in each city," replied the oracle. Even priests, in those ages, could, it seems, allow salvation to those of a different communion. The Romans commonly adopted the Gods of the conquered people; and never disputed the attributes of those local and national deities in whose territories they resided. . . .

The intolerance of almost all religions which have maintained the unity of God is as remarkable as the contrary principle of polytheists. The implacable narrow spirit of the Jews is well known. Mahometanism set out with still more bloody principles; and even to this day, deals out damnation, though not fire and faggot, to all other sects. And if, among Christians, the English and Dutch have embraced the principles of toleration, this singularity has proceeded from the steady resolution of the civil magistrate, in opposition to the continued efforts of priest and bigots. . . .

So sociable is polytheism, that the utmost fierceness and aversion which it meets with in an opposite religion is scarcely able to disgust it, and keep it at a distance. Augustus praised extremely the reserve of his grandson, Caius Caesar, when this latter prince, passing by Jerusalem, deigned not to sacrifice according to the Jewish law. But for what reason did Augustus so much approve of this conduct? Only because that religion was by the Pagans esteemed ignoble and barbarous. . . .

Section X

. . . Where the deity is represented as infinitely superior to mankind, this belief, though altogether just, is apt, when joined with superstitious terrors, to sink the human mind into the lowest submission and abasement, and to represent the monkish virtues of mortification, penance, humility, and passive suffering, as the only qualities which are acceptable to him. . . . The heroes in paganism correspond exactly to the saints in popery and holy dervishes in Mahometanism. The place of Hercules, Theseus, Hector, Romulus, is now supplied by Dominic, Francis, Anthony, and Benedict. Instead of the destruction of monsters, the subduing of tyrants, the defense of our native country; whippings and fasting, cowardice and humility, abject submission and slavish obedience, are become the means of obtaining celestial honors among mankind. . . .

Bellarmine patiently and humbly allowed the fleas and other odious vermin to prey upon him. "We shall have heaven," said he, "to reward us for our sufferings; but these poor creatures have nothing but the enjoyment of the present life." Such difference is there between the maxims of a Greek hero and a Catholic saint.

Section XI

... Philosophy ... instead of regulating ... [religion], as they advance together, ... is at every turn perverted to serve the purposes of superstition. For besides the unavoidable incoherencies which must be reconciled and adjusted, one may safely affirm that all popular theology, especially the scholastic, has a kind of appetite for absurdity and contradiction. If that theology went not beyond reason and common sense, her doctrines would appear too easy and familiar. Amazement must of necessity be raised; mystery affected; darkness and obscurity sought after; and a foundation of merit afforded the devout votaries, who desire an opportunity of subduing their rebellious reason, by the belief of the most unintelligible sophisms. . . .

Section XII

... It must be allowed that the Roman Catholics are a very learned sect, and that no one communion but that of the Church of England can dispute their being the most learned of all the Christian Churches. Yet Averroes, the famous Arabian, who, no doubt, has heard of the Egyptian superstitions, declares that of all religions the most absurd and nonsensical is that whose votaries eat, after having created, their deity.

I believe, indeed, that there is no tenet in all paganism which would give so fair a scope to ridicule as this of the *real presence.* For it is so absurd, that it eludes the force of all argument.... In a future age, it will probably become difficult to persuade some nations that any human, two-legged creature could ever embrace such principles....

Upon the whole, the greatest and most observable differences between a *traditional mythological* religion and a *systematical scholastical* one, are two. The former is often more reasonable, as consisting only of a multitude of stories, which, however groundless, imply no express absurdity and demonstrative contradiction; and sits also so easy and light on men's minds, that, though it may be as universally received, it happily makes no such deep impression on the affections and understanding....

Section XIV

... Virtuous conduct is deemed no more than what we owe to society and to ourselves. In all this a superstitious man finds nothing which he has properly performed for the sake of his deity, or which can peculiarly recommend him to the divine favor and protection. He considers not that the most genuine method of serving the divinity is by promoting the happiness of his creatures. He still looks out for some more immediate service of the supreme-being, in order to allay those terrors with which he is haunted. And any practice recommended to him which either serves to no purpose in life, or offers the strongest violence to his natural inclinations, that practice he will the more readily embrace. . . . If he fasts a day, or gives himself a sound whipping, this has a direct reference, in his opinion, to the service of God. No other motive could engage him to such austerities. By these distinguished marks of devotion he has now acquired the divine favor; and may expect, in recompense, protection and safety in this world and eternal happiness in the next.

Hence the greatest crimes have been found, in many instances, compatible with a superstitious piety and devotion. Hence it is justly regarded as unsafe to draw any certain inference in favor of a man's morals from the fervor or strictness of his religious exercises, even though he himself believes them sincere. Nay, it has been observed that enormities of the blackest dye have been rather apt to produce superstitious terrors, and increase the religious passion. . . .

. . . After the commission of crimes, there arise remorse and secret horrors, which give no rest to the mind, but make it have recourse to religious rites and ceremonies, as expiations of its offenses. Whatever weakens or disorders the internal frame promotes the interests of superstition; and nothing is more destructive to them than a manly steady virtue, which either preserves us from disastrous, melancholy accidents, or teaches us to bear them. During such calm sunshine of the mind, these specters of false divinity never make their appearance. . . .

Section XV

. . . In life . . . good and ill are universally intermingled and confounded; happiness and misery, wisdom and folly, virtue and vice. Nothing is purely and entirely of a piece. All advantages are attended with disadvantages. A universal compensation prevails in all conditions of being and existence. And it is not possible for us, by our most chimerical wishes, to form the idea of a station or situation altogether desirable. . . .

The more exquisite any good is, of which a small specimen is afforded us, the sharper is the evil allied to it; and few exceptions are found to this uniform law of nature. The most sprightly wit borders on madness; the highest effusions of joy produce the deepest melancholy. . . . As the good, the great, the sublime, the ravishing, are found eminently in the genuine principles of theism; it may be expected, from the analogy of nature, that the base, the absurd, the mean, the terrifying, will be discovered equally in religious fictions and chimeras. . . .

Survey most nations and most ages. Examine the religious principles which have, in fact, prevailed in the world. You will scarcely be persuaded that they are other than sick men's dreams; or perhaps will regard them more as the playsome whimsies of monkeys in human shape than the serious, positive, dogmatical asseverations of a being who dignifies himself with the name of rational.

Hear the verbal protestations of all men. Nothing they are so certain of as their religious tenets. Examine their lives. You will scarcely think that they repose the smallest confidence in them. . . .

No theological absurdities so glaring as have not, sometimes, been embraced by men of the greatest and most cultivated understanding. No religious precepts so rigorous as have not been adopted by the most voluptuous and most abandoned of men. . . .

What so pure as some of the morals included in some theological systems? What so corrupt as some of the practices to which these systems give rise?

The comfortable views exhibited by the belief of futurity are ravishing and delightful. But how quickly they vanish on the appearance of its terrors, which keep a more firm and durable possession of the human mind!

The whole is a riddle, an enigma, an inexplicable mystery. Doubt, uncertainty, suspense of judgment, appear the only result of our most accurate scrutiny concerning this subject. But such is the frailty of human reason, and such the irresistible contagion of opinion, that even this deliberate doubt could scarcely be upheld, did we not enlarge our view, and, opposing one species of superstition to another, set them a quarrelling; while we ourselves, during their fury and contention, happily make our escape into the calm, though obscure, regions of philosophy.

Dialogues Concerning Natural Religion

(1779)

What follows is a dialogue between:

- PHILO, a skeptical philosopher who believes conventional religion does more harm than good;

- CLEANTHES, who wants to reconcile Christian faith and reason, who bases his arguments on experience alone, and who rejects logical proofs of God's existence, and;

- DEMEA, a traditional Christian whose religion is based on faith, but who also accepts logical proofs of God's existence.

It is believed that Philo speaks for Hume both in general and in the famous refutations of the philosophical "proofs" for God's existence, the argument from design (the world shows the handiwork of a master designer) and the ontological argument (to be perfect, God must be).

———— ❦ ————

Philo (skeptic):

"... Let us become thoroughly sensible of the weakness, blindness, and narrow limits of human reason; let us duly consider its uncertainty and endless contrarieties, even in subjects of common life and practice; let the errors and deceits of our very senses be set before us; the insuperable difficulties which attend first principles in all systems; the contradictions which adhere to the very ideas of matter, cause and effect, extension, space, time, motion, and, in a word, quantity of all kinds, the object of the only science that can fairly pretend to any certainty or evidence. . . .

"... When we look beyond human affairs and the properties of the surrounding bodies, when we carry our speculations into the two eternities, before and after the present state of things: into the creation and formation of the universe, the existence and properties of spirits, the powers and operations of one universal Spirit existing without beginning and without end, omnipotent, omniscient, immutable, infinite, and incomprehensible—we must be far removed from the smallest tendency to skepticism not to be apprehensive that we have here got quite beyond the reach of our faculties. So long as we confine our speculations to trade, or morals, or politics, or criticism, we make appeals, every moment, to common sense and experience, which strengthen our philosophical conclusions and remove at least in part, the suspicion which we so justly entertain with regard to every reasoning that is very subtle and refined. But, in theological reasonings, we have not this advantage. . . ." (Part I)

CLEANTHES (Christian reconciler of faith and reason with an emphasis on experience):

"Not to lose any time in circumlocutions," said Cleanthes, . . . "I shall briefly explain how I conceive this matter. Look round the world, contemplate the whole and every part of it. You will find it to be nothing but one great machine, subdivided into an infinite number of lesser machines, which again admit of subdivisions to a degree beyond what human senses and faculties can trace and explain. All these various machines, and even their most minute parts, are adjusted to each other with an accuracy which ravishes into admiration all men who have ever contemplated them. The curious adapting of means to ends, throughout all nature, resembles exactly, though it much exceeds, the productions of human contrivance; of human designs, thought, wisdom, and intelligence. Since, therefore, the effects resemble each other, we are led to infer, by all the rules of analogy, that the causes also resemble; and that the Author of Nature is somewhat similar to the mind of man, though possessed of much larger faculties, proportioned to the grandeur of the work which he has executed. By this argument *a posteriori*, and by this argument alone, do we prove at once the existence of a Deity, and his similarity to human mind and intelligence."

DEMEA (Christian with emphasis on faith but also on logic):

"I shall be so free, Cleanthes," said Demea, "as to tell you, that . . . I . . . [do] not approve of your conclusion concerning the similarity of the Deity to men; still less can I approve of the mediums by which you endeavor to establish it. What! No demonstration of the Being of God! No abstract arguments! No proofs *a priori*! Are these, which have hitherto been so much insisted on by philosophers, all fallacy, all sophism? Can we reach no further in this subject than experience and probability? I will not say that this is betraying the cause of a Deity; but surely . . . you give advantages to Atheists. . . ."

PHILO (skeptic):

"What I chiefly scruple in this subject," said Philo, "is not so much that all religious arguments are by Cleanthes reduced to experience, as that they appear not to be even the most certain and irrefragable of that inferior kind. That a stone will fall, that fire will burn, that the earth has solidity, we have observed a thousand and a thousand times; and when any new instance of this nature is presented, we draw without hesitation the accustomed inference. The exact similarity of the cases gives us a perfect assurance of a similar event; and a stronger evidence is never desired nor sought after. But wherever you depart, in the least, from the similarity of the cases, you diminish proportionally the evidence; and may at last bring it to a very weak analogy, which is confessedly liable to error and uncertainty. After having experienced the circulation of the blood in human creatures, we make no doubt that it takes place in Titius and Maevius. But from its circulation in frogs and fishes, it is only a presumption, though a strong one, from analogy, that it takes place in men and other animals. The analogical reasoning is much weaker, when we infer the circulation of the sap in vegetables from our experience that the blood circulates in animals; and those, who hastily followed that imperfect analogy, are found, by more accurate experiments, to have been mistaken.

"If we see a house, Cleanthes, we conclude, with the greatest certainty, that it had an architect or builder because this is precisely that species of effect which we have experienced to proceed from that species of cause. But surely you will not affirm that the universe bears such a resemblance to a house that we can with the same certainty infer a similar cause, or that the analogy is here entire and perfect. The dissimilitude is so striking that the utmost you can here pretend to is a guess. . . .

"[In addition,] thought, design, intelligence, such as we discover in men and other animals, is no more than one of the springs and principles of the universe, as well as heat or cold, attraction or repulsion, and a hundred others which fall under daily observation. It is an active cause by which some particular parts of nature, we find, produce alterations on other parts. But can a conclusion, with any propriety, be transferred from parts to the whole? Does not the great disproportion bar all comparison and inference? From observing the growth of a hair, can we learn anything concerning the generation of a man? Would the manner of a leaf's blowing, even though perfectly known, afford us any instruction concerning the vegetation of a tree?

"But allowing that we were to take the operations of one part of nature upon another for the foundation of our judgment concerning the origin of the whole (which never can be admitted), yet why select so minute, so weak, so bounded a principle as the reason and design of animals is found to be upon this planet? What peculiar privilege has this little agitation of the brain which we call thought, that we must thus make it the model of the whole universe? Our partiality in our own favor does indeed present it on all occasions, but sound philosophy ought carefully to guard against so natural an illusion. . . .

". . . Is there any reasonable ground to conclude that the inhabitants of other planets possess thought, intelligence, reason, or anything similar to these faculties in men? When nature has so extremely diversified her manner of operation in this small globe, can we imagine that she incessantly copies herself throughout so immense a universe? And if thought, as we may well suppose, be confined merely to this narrow corner and has even there so limited a sphere of action, with what propriety can we assign it for the original cause of all things? . . .

"A very small part of this great system, during a very short time, is very imperfectly discovered to us; and do we thence pronounce decisively concerning the origin of the whole? . . .

"And can you blame me, Cleanthes, if I here imitate the prudent reserve of Simonides, who, according to the noted story, being asked by Hiero, *What God was*? desired a day to think of it, and then two days more; and after that manner continually prolonged the term, without ever bringing in his definition or description? Could you even blame me if I had answered, at first, that I did not know, and was sensible that this subject lay vastly beyond the reach of my faculties? You might cry out skeptic . . . as much as you pleased: but, having found in so many other subjects much more familiar the imperfections and even contradictions of human reason, I never should expect any success from its feeble conjectures in a subject so sublime and so remote from the sphere of our observation. . . ." (Part II)

CLEANTHES (Christian reconciler of faith and reason, with emphasis on experience):

"It seems strange to me," said Cleanthes, "that you, Demea, who are so sincere in the cause of religion, should still maintain the mysterious, incomprehensible nature of the Deity, and should insist so strenuously that he has no manner of likeness or resemblance to human creatures. The Deity, I can readily allow, possesses many powers and attributes of which we can have no comprehension; but if our ideas, so far as they go, be not just and adequate, and correspondent to his real nature, I know not what there is in this subject worth insisting on. Is the name, without any meaning, of such mighty importance? Or how do you mystics, who maintain the absolute incomprehensibility of the Deity, differ from skeptics or atheists, who assert that the first cause of all is unknown and unintelligible? . . ."

DEMEA (Christian with emphasis on faith but also on logic):

"Who could imagine," replied Demea, "that Cleanthes, the calm, philosophical Cleanthes, would attempt to refute his antagonists, by affixing a nick-name to them; and like the common bigots and inquisitors of the age, have recourse to invective and declamation, instead of reasoning? Or does he not perceive, that these topics are easily retorted, and that anthropomorphite is an appellation as invidious, and implies as dangerous consequences, as the epithet of mystic, with which he has honored us? In reality, Cleanthes, consider what it is you assert, when you represent the deity as similar to a human mind and understanding. . . . New opinions, new passions, new affections, new feelings arise, which continually diversify the . . . [human] mental scene, and produce in it the greatest variety, and most rapid succession imaginable. How is this compatible, with that perfect immutability and simplicity, which all true theists ascribe to the deity?"

PHILO (skeptic):

[Also addressing Cleanthes: "And] . . . how . . . shall we satisfy ourselves concerning the cause of that Being whom you suppose the Author of nature, or, according to your system of anthropomorphism, the ideal world. . . . If the material world rests upon a similar ideal world, this ideal world must rest upon some other, and so on without end. It were better, therefore, never to look beyond the present material world. . . . (Part IV)

"And why not become a perfect anthropomorphite? Why not assert the deity or deities to be corporeal, and to have eyes, a nose, mouth, ears, etc.? Epicurus maintained that no man had ever seen reason but in a human figure; therefore, the gods must have a human figure. And this argument, which is deservedly so much ridiculed by Cicero, becomes, according to you, solid and philosophical.

"In a word, Cleanthes, a man who follows your hypothesis is able, perhaps, to assert or conjecture that the universe sometime arose from something like design; but beyond that position he cannot ascertain one single circumstance, and is left afterwards to fix every point of his theology by the utmost license of fancy and hypothesis. This world, for aught he knows, is very faulty and imperfect, compared to a superior standard, and was only the first rude essay of some infant deity who afterwards abandoned it, ashamed of his lame performance; it is the work only of some dependent, inferior deity, and is the object of derision to his superiors; it is the production of old age and dotage in some superannuated deity, and ever since his death has run on at adventures, from the first impulse and active force which it received from him. You justly give signs of horror, Demea, at these strange suppositions; but these, and a thousand more of the same kind, are Cleanthes's suppositions, not mine. From the moment the attributes of the Deity are supposed finite, all these have place. And I cannot, for my part, think that so wild and unsettled a system of theology is, in any respect, preferable to none at all. . . . (Part V)

. . . Philo continued. . . . "A tree bestows order and organization on that tree which springs from it . . . ; an animal in the same manner on its offspring; a bird on its nest; and instances of this kind are even more frequent in the world than those of order which arise from reason and contrivance. To say that all this order in animals and vegetables proceeds ultimately from design is begging the question; nor can that great point be ascertained otherwise than by proving, *a priori*, both that order is, from its nature, inseparably attached to thought and that it can never of itself or from original unknown principles, belong to matter. . . .

". . . Why an orderly system may not be spun from the belly as well as from the brain, it will be difficult for . . . Cleanthes to give a satisfactory reason. . . . (Part VII)

"What you ascribe to the fertility of my invention, . . . Cleanthes, is entirely owing to the nature of the subject. In subjects adapted to the narrow compass of human reason there is commonly but one determination which carries probability or conviction with it; and to a man of sound judgment, all other suppositions, but that one, appear entirely absurd and chimerical. But in such questions as the present, a hundred contradictory views may preserve a kind of imperfect analogy; and invention has here full scope to exert itself. Without any great effort of thought, I believe that I could, in an instant, propose other systems of cosmogony, which would have some faint appearance of truth, though it is a thousand, a million to one, if either yours or any one of mine be the true system. . . .

"All religious systems, it is confessed, are subject to great and insuperable difficulties. Each disputant triumphs in his turn, while he carries on an offensive war, and exposes the absurdities, barbarities, and pernicious tenets of his antagonist. But all of them, on the whole, prepare a complete triumph for the *skeptic*, who tells them, that no system ought ever to be embraced with regard to such subjects; for this plain reason that no absurdity ought ever to be assented to with regard to any subject. A total suspense of judgment is here our only reasonable resource. And if every attack, as is commonly observed, and no defense, among theologians is successful, how complete must be his victory, who remains always, with all mankind, on the offensive, and has himself no fixed station or abiding city, which he is ever, on any occasion, obliged to defend?" (Part VIII)

DEMEA (Christian with emphasis on faith, but also on logic):

"But if so many difficulties attend the argument *a posteriori*," said Demea, "had we not better adhere to that simple and sublime argument *a priori* which, by offering to us infallible demonstration, cuts off at once all doubt and difficulty? By this argument, too, we may prove the infinity of the Divine attributes, which, I am afraid, can never be ascertained with certainty from any other topic. For how can an effect, which either is finite, or, for aught we know, may be so—how can such an effect, I say, prove an infinite cause? The unity, too, of the Divine Nature, it is very difficult, if not absolutely impossible, to deduce merely from contemplating the works of nature; nor will the uniformity alone of the plan, even were it allowed, give us any assurance of that attribute. Whereas the argument *a priori*. . . ."

CLEANTHES (Christian reconciler of religion and reason with an emphasis on experience):

"You seem to reason, Demea," interposed Cleanthes, "as if those advantages and conveniences in the abstract argument were full proofs of its solidity. But it is first proper, in my opinion, to determine what argument of this nature you choose to insist on; and we shall afterwards, from itself, better than from its useful consequences, endeavor to determine what value we ought to put upon it."

DEMEA (Christian with emphasis on faith but also on logic):

"The argument," replied Demea, "which I would insist on, is the common one. Whatever exists must have a cause or reason of its existence; it being absolutely impossible for anything to produce itself, or be the cause of its own existence. In mounting up, therefore, from effects to causes, we must either go on in tracing an infinite succession, without any ultimate cause at all; or must at last have recourse to some ultimate cause, that is necessarily existent: Now, that the first supposition is absurd, may be thus proved. In the infinite chain or succession of causes and effects, each single effect is determined to exist by the power and efficacy of that cause which immediately preceded; but the whole eternal chain or succession, taken together, is not determined or caused by anything; and yet it is evident that it requires a cause or reason, as much as any particular object which begins to exist in time. The question is still reasonable, why this particular succession of causes existed from eternity, and not any other succession, or no succession at all. If there be no necessarily existent being, any supposition which can be formed is equally possible; nor is there any more absurdity in Nothing's having existed from eternity, than there is in that succession of causes which constitutes the universe. What was it, then, which determined Something to exist rather than Nothing, and bestowed being on a particular possibility, exclusive of the rest? External causes, there are supposed to be none. Chance is a word without a meaning. Was it Nothing? But that can never produce anything. We must, therefore, have recourse to a necessarily existent Being, who carries the reason of his existence in himself, and who cannot be supposed not to exist, without an express contradiction. There is, consequently, such a Being; that is, there is a deity."

CLEANTHES (Christian reconciler of faith and reason, with emphasis on experience):

"I shall not leave it to Philo," said Cleanthes, "though I know that . . . [raising] objections is his chief delight, to point out the weakness of . . . [Demea's endorsement of a purely logical proof, unrelated to experience, for the existence of God]. It seems to me so obviously ill-grounded, and at the same time of so little consequence to the cause of true piety and religion, that I shall myself venture to show the fallacy of it.

"I shall begin with observing, that there is an evident absurdity in pretending to demonstrate a matter of fact, or to prove it by any arguments *a priori*. Nothing is demonstrable unless the contrary implies a contradiction. Nothing, that is distinctly conceivable, implies a contradiction. Whatever we conceive as existent, we can also conceive as non-existent. There is no being, therefore, whose non-existence implies a contradiction. Consequently there is no being, whose existence is demonstrable. I propose this argument as entirely decisive, and am willing to rest the whole controversy upon it.

"It is pretended that the Deity is a necessarily existent being; and this necessity of his existence is attempted to be explained by asserting, that if we knew his whole essence or nature, we should perceive it to be as impossible for him not to exist, as for twice two not to be four. But it is evident that this can never happen, while our faculties remain the same as at present. It will still be possible for us, at any time, to conceive the non-existence of what we formerly conceived to exist. . . . The words, therefore, necessary existence, have no meaning; or, which is the same thing, none that is consistent. . . ."

PHILO (skeptic):

"Though the reasonings which you have urged, Cleanthes, may well excuse me," said Philo, "from starting any further difficulties, yet I cannot forbear insisting still upon another topic. It is observed by arithmeticians, that the products of 9, compose always either 9, or some lesser product of 9, if you add together all the characters of which any of the former products is composed. Thus, of 18, 27, 36, which are products of 9, you make 9 by adding 1 to 8, 2 to 7, 3 to 6. Thus, 369 is a product also of 9; and if you add 3, 6, and 9, you make 18, a lesser product of 9. To a superficial observer, so wonderful a regularity may be admired as the effect either of chance or design; but a skillful algebraist immediately concludes it to be the work of necessity, and demonstrates, that it must forever result from the nature of these numbers. Is it not probable, I ask, that the whole economy of the universe is conducted by a like necessity, though no human algebra can furnish a key which solves the difficulty? And instead of admiring the order of natural beings, may it not happen, that, could we penetrate into the intimate nature of bodies, we should clearly see why it was absolutely impossible they could ever admit of any other disposition? So dangerous is it to introduce this idea of necessity into the present question! And so naturally does it afford an inference directly opposite to the religious hypothesis!

"But dropping all these abstractions," continued Philo, "and confining ourselves to more familiar topics, I shall venture to add an observation, that the argument *a priori* has seldom been found very convincing, except to people of a metaphysical head, who have accustomed themselves to abstract reasoning, and who, finding from mathematics, that the understanding frequently leads to truth through obscurity, and, contrary to first appearances, have transferred the same habit of thinking to subjects where it ought not to have place. Other people, even of good sense and the best inclined to religion, feel always some deficiency in such arguments, though they are not perhaps able to explain distinctly where it lies—a certain proof that men ever did, and ever will derive their religion from other sources than from this species of reasoning. (Part IX)

". . . I am indeed persuaded," said Philo, "that the best, and indeed the only method of bringing everyone to a due sense of religion, is by just representations of the misery and wickedness of men. And for that purpose a talent of eloquence and strong imagery is more requisite than that of reasoning and argument. For is it necessary to prove what everyone feels within himself? It is only necessary to make us feel it, if possible, more intimately and sensibly. . . .

"Observe too," says Philo, "the curious artifices of nature, in order to embitter the life of every living being. The stronger prey upon the weaker, and keep them in perpetual terror and anxiety. The weaker too, in their turn, often prey upon the stronger, and vex and molest them without relaxation. Consider that innumerable race of insects, which either are bred on the body of each animal, or, flying about, infix their stings in him. These insects have others still less than themselves, which torment them. And thus on each hand, before and behind, above and below, every animal is surrounded with enemies, which incessantly seek his misery and destruction."

DEMEA (Christian with emphasis on faith but also on logic):

"Man alone," said Demea, "seems to be, in part, an exception to this rule. For by combination in society, he can easily master lions, tigers, and bears, whose greater strength and agility naturally enable them to prey upon him."

PHILO (skeptic):

"On the contrary, it is here chiefly," cried Philo, "that the uniform and equal maxims of nature are most apparent. Man, it is true, can, by combination, surmount all his real enemies, and become master of the whole animal creation; but does he not immediately raise up to himself imaginary enemies, the demons of his fancy, who haunt him with superstitious terrors, and blast every enjoyment of life? His pleasure, as he imagines, becomes in their eyes a crime; his food and repose give them umbrage and offense; his very sleep and dreams furnish new materials to anxious fear; and even death, his refuge from every other ill, presents only the dread of endless and innumerable woes. Nor does the wolf molest more the timid flock, than superstition does the anxious breast of wretched mortals.

"Besides, consider, Demea: This very society, by which we surmount those wild beasts, our natural enemies, what new enemies does it not raise to us?

What woe and misery does it not occasion? Man is the greatest enemy of man. Oppression, injustice, contempt, contumely, violence, sedition, war, calumny, treachery, fraud—by these they mutually torment each other, and they would soon dissolve that society which they had formed, were it not for the dread of still greater ills, which must attend their separation."

DEMEA (Christian with emphasis on faith but also on logic):

"But though these external insults," said Demea, "from animals, from men, from all the elements, which assault us, form a frightful catalog of woes, they are nothing in comparison of those which arise within ourselves, from the distempered condition of our mind and body. How many lie under the lingering torment of diseases? Hear the pathetic enumeration of the great poet."

> Intestine stone and ulcer, colic-pangs,
> Demoniac frenzy, moping melancholy,
> And moon-struck madness, pining atrophy,
> Marasmus, and wide-wasting pestilence.
> Dire was the tossing, deep the groans:
>   Despair
> Tended the sick, busiest from couch to
>   couch.
> And over them triumphant Death his
>   dart

Shook: but delay'd to strike, though of-
　　ten invok'd
With vows, as their chief good and final
　　hope.

—John Milton: *Paradise Lost*, Book XI

"The disorders of the mind," continued Demea,
"though more secret, are not perhaps less dismal and
vexatious. Remorse, shame, anguish, rage, disappointment, anxiety, fear, dejection, despair—who has ever
passed through life without cruel inroads from these
tormentors? How many have scarcely ever felt any
better sensations? Labor and poverty, so abhorred by
everyone, are the certain lot of the far greater number; and those few privileged persons who enjoy ease
and opulence, never reach contentment or true felicity. All the goods of life united would not make a
very happy man, but all the ills united would make a
wretch indeed; and any one of them almost (and who
can be free from every one?) nay, often the absence of
one good (and who can possess all?) is sufficient to
render life ineligible.

"Were a stranger to drop on a sudden into this world,
I would show him, as a specimen of its ills, a hospital
full of diseases, a prison crowded with malefactors and
debtors, a field of battle strewed with carcasses, a fleet
foundering in the ocean, a nation languishing under
tyranny, famine, or pestilence. To turn the gay side of

life to him, and give him a notion of its pleasures—whither should I conduct him? To a ball, to an opera, to court? He might justly think that I was only showing him a diversity of distress and sorrow."

Philo (skeptic):

"There is no evading such striking instances," said Philo, "but by apologies, which still further aggravate the charge. Why have all men, I ask, in all ages, complained incessantly of the miseries of life? . . . They have no just reason, says one: these complaints proceed only from their discontented, repining, anxious disposition. . . . And can there possibly, I reply, be a more certain foundation of misery, than such a wretched temper?

"But if they were really as unhappy as they pretend, says my antagonist, why do they remain in life? . . .

"Not satisfied with life, afraid of death—this is the secret chain, say I, that holds us. We are terrified, not bribed to the continuance of our existence.

"It is only a false delicacy, he may insist, which a few refined spirits indulge, and which has spread these complaints among the whole race of mankind. . . . And what is this delicacy, I ask, which you blame? Is it anything but a greater sensibility to all the pleasures and pains of life? And if the man of a delicate, refined temper, by being so much more alive than the rest of the world, is only so much more unhappy, what judgment must we form in general of human life?

"Let men remain at rest, says our adversary, and they will be easy. They are willing artificers of their own misery. . . . No! reply I: an anxious languor follows their repose; disappointment, vexation, trouble, their activity and ambition."

CLEANTHES (The Reconciler of Faith and Reason):

"I can observe something like what you mention in some others," replied Cleanthes, "but I confess I feel little or nothing of it in myself, and hope that it is not so common as you represent it."

DEMEA (Christian with emphasis on faith but also on logic):

"If you feel not human misery yourself," cried Demea, "I congratulate you on so happy a singularity. Others, seemingly the most prosperous, have not been ashamed to vent their complaints in the most melancholy strains. Let us attend to the great, the fortunate emperor, Charles V, when, tired with human grandeur, he resigned all his extensive dominions into the hands of his son. In the last harangue which he made on that memorable occasion, he publicly avowed, that the greatest prosperities which he had ever enjoyed, had been mixed with so many adversities, that he might truly say he had never enjoyed any satisfaction or contentment. But did the retired life, in which he sought for shelter, afford him any greater happiness?

If we may credit his son's account, his repentance commenced the very day of his resignation.

"Cicero's fortune, from small beginnings, rose to the greatest luster and renown; yet what pathetic complaints of the ills of life do his familiar letters, as well as philosophical discourses, contain? And suitably to his own experience, he introduces Cato, the great, the fortunate Cato, protesting in his old age, that had he a new life in his offer, he would reject the present.

"Ask yourself, ask any of your acquaintance, whether they would live over again the last ten or twenty years of their life. No! but the next twenty, they say, will be better:

> And from the dregs of life, hope to receive
> What the first sprightly running could
> > not give.

—John Dryden, *Aureng-Zebe*, Act IV, SC. I.

"Thus at last they find (such is the greatness of human misery, it reconciles even contradictions) that they complain at once of the shortness of life, and of its vanity and sorrow."

PHILO (skeptic):

"And is it possible, Cleanthes," said Philo, "that after all these reflections, and infinitely more, which might be suggested, you can still persevere in your anthropomorphism, and assert the moral attributes of the Deity, his justice, benevolence, mercy, and rectitude, to be of the same nature with these virtues in human creatures? His power, we allow, is infinite; whatever he wills is executed; but neither man nor any other animal is happy; therefore, he does not will their happiness. His wisdom is infinite; He is never mistaken in choosing the means to any end; but the course of nature tends not to human or animal felicity; therefore it is not established for that purpose. Through the whole compass of human knowledge, there are no inferences more certain and infallible than these. In what respect, then, do his benevolence and mercy resemble the benevolence and mercy of men?

"Epicurus's old questions are yet unanswered.

"Is he willing to prevent evil, but not able? Then is he impotent. Is he able, but not willing? Then is he malevolent. Is he both able and willing? Whence then is evil?

"You ascribe, Cleanthes (and I believe justly) a purpose and intention to nature. But what, I beseech you, is the object of that curious artifice and machinery, which she has displayed in all animals—the preservation alone of individuals, and propagation of the species. It seems enough for her purpose, if such a rank be barely upheld in the universe, without any care or concern for the happiness of the members that compose it. No resource for this purpose: no machinery, in order merely to give pleasure or ease; no fund of pure joy and contentment; no indulgence, without some want or necessity accompanying it. At least, the few phenomena of this nature are overbalanced by opposite phenomena of still greater importance.

"Our sense of music, harmony, and indeed beauty of all kinds, gives satisfaction, without being absolutely necessary to the preservation and propagation of the species. But what racking pains, on the other hand, arise from gouts, gravels (kidney stones), megrims (migraines), toothaches, rheumatisms, where the injury to the animal machinery is either small or incurable? Mirth, laughter, play, frolic, seem gratuitous satisfactions, which have no further tendency; spleen, melancholy, discontent, superstition, are pains of the same nature. How then does the Divine benevolence display itself, in the sense of you anthropomorphites? None but we mystics, as you were pleased to call us, can account for this strange mixture of phenomena, by deriving it from attributes, infinitely perfect, but incomprehensible."

Cleanthes (Christian reconciler of faith and reason with emphasis on experience):

"And have you, at last," said Cleanthes smiling, "betrayed your intentions, Philo? Your long agreement with Demea did indeed a little surprise me, but I find you were all the while erecting a concealed battery against me. And I must confess that you have now fallen upon a subject worthy of your noble spirit of opposition and controversy. If you can make out the present point, and prove mankind to be unhappy or corrupted, there is an end at once of all religion. . . ."

DEMEA (Christian with emphasis on faith but also on logic):

"You take umbrage very easily," replied Demea, "at opinions the most innocent, and the most generally received, even amongst the religious and devout themselves: and nothing can be more surprising than to find a topic like this—concerning the wickedness and misery of man—charged with no less than atheism and profaneness. Have not all pious divines and preachers, who have indulged their rhetoric on so fertile a subject, have they not easily, I say, given a solution of any difficulties which may attend it? This world is but a point in comparison of the universe; this life but a moment in comparison of eternity. The present evil phenomena, therefore, are rectified in other regions, and in some future period of existence. And the eyes of men, being then opened to larger views of things, see the whole connection of general laws, and trace, with adoration, the benevolence and rectitude of the Deity through all the mazes and intricacies of his providence."

Cleanthes (Christian reconciler of faith and reason with emphasis on experience):

"No!" replied Cleanthes, "no! These arbitrary suppositions can never be admitted, contrary to matter of fact, visible and uncontroverted. Whence can any cause be known but from its known effects? Whence can any hypothesis be proved but from the apparent phenomena? To establish one hypothesis upon another is building entirely in the air; and the utmost we ever attain, by these conjectures and fictions is to ascertain the bare possibility of our opinion, but never can we, upon such terms, establish its reality.

"The only method of supporting Divine benevolence—and it is what I willingly embrace—is to deny absolutely the misery and wickedness of man. Your representations are exaggerated; your melancholy views mostly fictitious; your inferences contrary to fact and experience. Health is more common than sickness; pleasure than pain; happiness than misery. And for one vexation which we meet with, we attain, upon computation, a hundred enjoyments."

Philo (skeptic):

"Admitting your position," replied Philo, "which yet is extremely doubtful, you must at the same time allow, that if pain be less frequent than pleasure, it is infinitely more violent and durable. One hour of it is often able to outweigh a day, a week, a month of our common insipid enjoyments; and how many days, weeks, and months, are passed by several in the most acute torments? Pleasure, scarcely in one instance, is ever able to reach ecstasy and rapture; and in no one instance can it continue for any time at its highest pitch and altitude. The spirits evaporate, the nerves relax, the fabric is disordered, and the enjoyment quickly degenerates into fatigue and uneasiness. But pain often, good God, how often! rises to torture and agony; and the longer it continues, it becomes still more genuine agony and torture. Patience is exhausted, courage languishes, melancholy seizes us, and nothing terminates our misery but the removal of its cause, or another event, which is the sole cure of all evil, but which, from our natural folly, we regard with still greater horror and consternation.

"But not to insist upon these topics," continued Philo, "though most obvious, certain, and important, I must use the freedom to admonish you, Cleanthes, that you have put the controversy upon a most dangerous issue, and are unawares introducing a total skepticism into the most essential articles of natural and revealed theology. What! No method of fixing a just foundation for religion unless we allow the happiness of human life, and maintain a continued existence even in this world, with all our present pains, infirmities, vexations, and follies, to be eligible and desirable! But this is contrary to everyone's feeling and experience; it is contrary to an authority so established as nothing can subvert. No decisive proofs can ever be produced against this authority; nor is it possible for you to compute, estimate, and compare, all the pains and all the pleasures in the lives of all men and of all animals; and thus, by your resting the whole system of religion on a point, which, from its very nature, must forever be uncertain, you tacitly confess, that that system is equally uncertain.

"But allowing you what never will be believed, at least what you never possibly can prove, that animal, or at least human happiness, in this life, exceeds its misery, you have yet done nothing; for this is not, by any means, what we expect from infinite power, infinite wisdom, and infinite goodness. Why is there any misery at all in the world? Not by chance, surely. From some cause then. Is it from the intention of the Deity? But he is perfectly benevolent. Is it contrary to his intention? But he is almighty. Nothing can shake the solidity of this reasoning, so short, so clear, so decisive, except we assert that these subjects exceed all human capacity, and that our common measures of truth and falsehood are not applicable to them—a topic which I have all along insisted on, but which you have, from the beginning, rejected with scorn and indignation.... (Part X)

"In short, I repeat the question: Is the world, considered in general, and as it appears to us in this life, different from what a man, or such a limited being, would, beforehand, expect from a very powerful, wise, and benevolent Deity? It must be strange prejudice to assert the contrary....

"There seem to be four circumstances, on which depend all, or the greatest part of the ills, that molest sensible creatures; and it is not impossible but all these circumstances may be necessary and unavoidable. We know so little beyond common life, or even of common life, that, with regard to the economy of a universe, there is no conjecture, however wild, which may not be just, nor any one, however plausible, which may not be erroneous. All that belongs to human understanding, in this deep ignorance and obscurity, is to be skeptical, or at least cautious, and not to admit of any hypothesis whatever, much less of any which is supported by no appearance of probability. Now, this I assert to be the case with regard to all the causes of evil, and the circumstances on which it depends. None of them appear to human reason in the least degree necessary or unavoidable, nor can we suppose them such, without the utmost license of imagination.

"The first circumstance which introduces evil, is that contrivance or economy of the animal creation, by which pains, as well as pleasures, are employed to excite all creatures to action, and make them vigilant in the great work of self-preservation. [But] ... pleasure alone, in its various degrees, seems to human understanding sufficient for this purpose....

". . . A capacity of pain would not alone produce pain, were it not for the second circumstance, viz., the conducting of the world by general laws; and this seems nowise necessary to a very perfect Being. It is true, if everything were conducted by particular volitions, the course of nature would be perpetually broken, and no man could employ his reason in the conduct of life. But might not other particular volitions remedy this inconvenience? In short, might not the Deity exterminate all ill, wherever it were to be found, and produce all good, without any preparation or long progress of causes and effects?

"Besides, we must consider, that, according to the present economy of the world, the course of nature, though supposed exactly regular, yet to us appears not so, and many events are uncertain, and many disappoint our expectations. Health and sickness, calm and tempest, with an infinite number of other accidents, whose causes are unknown and variable, have a great influence both on the fortunes of particular persons and on the prosperity of public societies; and indeed all human life, in a manner, depends on such accidents. A being, therefore, who knows the secret springs of the universe, might easily, by particular volitions, turn all these accidents to the good of mankind, and render the whole world happy, without discovering himself in any operation. A fleet, whose purposes were salutary to society, might always meet with a fair wind. Good princes enjoy sound health and long life. Persons born to power and authority be framed with good tempers and virtuous dispositions. A few such events as these, regularly and wisely conducted, would change the face of the world, and yet would no more seem to disturb the course of nature, or confound human conduct, than the present economy of things, where the causes are secret, and variable, and compounded. Some small touches given to Caligula's brain in his infancy, might have converted him into a Trajan. One wave, a little higher than the rest, by burying Caesar and his fortune in the bottom of the ocean, might have restored liberty to a considerable part of mankind. There may, for aught we know, be good reasons why Providence interposes not in this manner, but they are unknown to us; and, though the mere supposition, that such reasons exist, may be sufficient to save the conclusion concerning the Divine attributes, yet surely it can never be sufficient to establish that conclusion.

"If everything in the universe be conducted by general laws, and if animals be rendered susceptible of pain, it scarcely seems possible but some ill must arise in the various shocks of matter, and the various concurrence and opposition of general laws; but this ill would be very rare, were it not for the third circumstance, which I proposed to mention, viz., the great frugality with which all powers and faculties are distributed to every particular being. . . .

"Wherever one power is increased, there is a proportional abatement in the others. Animals which excel in swiftness are commonly defective in force. Those which possess both are either imperfect in some of their senses, or are oppressed with the most craving wants. The human species, whose chief excellency is reason and sagacity, is of all others the most necessitous, and the most deficient in bodily advantages, without clothes, without arms, without food, without lodging, without any convenience of life, except what they owe to their own skill and industry.

"In short, nature seems to have formed an exact calculation of the necessities of her creatures, and, like a rigid master, has afforded them little more powers or endowments than what are strictly sufficient to supply those necessities. An indulgent parent would have bestowed a large stock, in order to guard against accidents, and secure the happiness and welfare of the creature in the most unfortunate concurrence of circumstances. . . .

"The author of nature is inconceivably powerful; his force is supposed great, if not altogether inexhaustible, nor is there any reason, as far as we can judge, to make him observe this strict frugality in his dealings with his creatures. It would have been better, were his power extremely limited, to have created fewer animals, and to have endowed these with more faculties for their happiness and preservation. . . .

"In order to cure most of the ills of human life, I require not that man should have the wings of the eagle, the swiftness of the stag, the force of the ox, the arms of the lion, the scales of the crocodile or rhinoceros; much less do I demand the sagacity of an angel or cherubim. I am contented to take an increase in one single power or faculty of his soul. Let him be endowed with a greater propensity to industry and labor; a more vigorous spring and activity of mind, a more constant bent to business and application. Let the whole species possess naturally an equal diligence with that which many individuals are able to attain by habit and reflection, and the most beneficial consequences, without any allay of ill, is the immediate and necessary result of this endowment. . . .

"The fourth circumstance, whence arises the misery and ill of the universe, is the inaccurate workmanship of all the springs and principles of the great machine of nature. . . . One would imagine, that this grand production had not received the last hand of the maker— so little finished is every part, and so coarse are the strokes with which it is executed. Thus, the winds are requisite to convey the vapors along the surface of the globe, and to assist men in navigation: but how often, rising up to tempests and hurricanes, do they become pernicious? Rains are necessary to nourish all the plants and animals of the earth; but how often are they defective? How often excessive? . . .

"On the concurrence, then, of these four circumstances, does all or the greatest part of natural evil depend. . . . What then shall we pronounce on this occasion? Shall we say that these circumstances are not necessary, and that they might easily have been altered in the contrivance of the universe? This decision seems too presumptuous for creatures so blind and ignorant. Let us be more modest in our conclusions. Let us allow, that, if the goodness of the Deity (I mean a goodness like the human) could be established on any tolerable reasons *a priori*, these phenomena, however untoward, would not be sufficient to subvert that principle, but might easily, in some unknown manner, be reconcilable to it. But let us still assert, that as this goodness is not antecedently established, but must be inferred from the phenomena, there can be no grounds for such an inference, while there are so many ills in the universe, and while these ills might so easily have been remedied, as far as human understanding can be allowed to judge on such a subject. . . .

"Look round this universe. What an immense profusion of beings, animated and organized, sensible and active! You admire this prodigious variety and fecundity. But inspect a little more narrowly these living existences, the only beings worth regarding. How hostile and destructive to each other! How insufficient all of them for their own happiness! How contemptible or odious to the spectator! The whole presents nothing but the idea of a blind nature, impregnated by a great vivifying principle, and pouring forth from her lap, without discernment or parental care, her maimed and abortive children!

"Here the Manichaean system occurs as a proper hypothesis to solve the difficulty: and no doubt, in some respects, it . . . has more probability than the common hypothesis, by giving a plausible account of the strange mixture of good and ill which appears in life. But if we consider, on the other hand, the perfect uniformity and agreement of the parts of the universe, we shall not discover in it any marks of the combat of a malevolent with a benevolent being. There is indeed an opposition of pains and pleasures in the feelings of sensible creatures; but are not all the operations of nature carried on by an opposition of principles, of hot and cold, moist and dry, light and heavy? The true conclusion is, that the original Source of all things is entirely indifferent to all these principles, and has no more regard to good above ill, than to heat above cold, or to drought above moisture, or to light above heavy.

"There may be four hypotheses . . . framed concerning the first causes of the universe: that they are endowed with perfect goodness; that they have perfect malice; that they are opposite, and have both goodness and malice; that they have neither goodness nor malice. Mixed phenomena can never prove the two former unmixed principles; and the uniformity and steadiness of general laws seem to oppose the third. The fourth, therefore, seems by far the most probable.

"What I have said concerning natural evil will apply to moral, with little or no variation; and we have no more reason to infer, that the rectitude of the Supreme Being resembles human rectitude, than that his benevolence resembles the human. Nay, it will be thought, that we have still greater cause to exclude from him moral sentiments, such as we feel them, since moral evil, in the opinion of many, is much more predominant above moral good than natural evil above natural good.

"But even though this should not be allowed, and though the virtue which is in mankind should be acknowledged much superior to the vice, yet so long as there is any vice at all in the universe, it will very much puzzle you anthropomorphites, how to account for it. You must assign a cause for it, without having recourse to the first cause. But as every effect must have a cause, and that cause another, you must either carry on the progression in infinitum, or rest on that original principle, who is the ultimate cause of all things. . . ."

CLEANTHES (Christian reconciler of faith and reason with emphasis on experience):

". . . Believe me, Demea, your friend Philo, from the beginning, has been amusing himself at both our expense; and it must be confessed, that the injudicious reasoning of our vulgar theology has given him but too just a handle of ridicule. The total infirmity of human reason, the absolute incomprehensibility of the Divine Nature, the great and universal misery, and still greater wickedness of men—these are strange topics, surely, to be so fondly cherished by orthodox divines and doctors. . . ."

PHILO (skeptic):

"Blame not so much," interposed Philo, "the ignorance of these reverend gentlemen. They know how to change their style with the times. Formerly, it was a most popular theological topic to maintain, that human life was vanity and misery, and to exaggerate all the ills and pains which are incident to men. But of late years, divines, we find, begin to retract this position and maintain, though still with some hesitation, that there are more goods than evils, more pleasures than pains, even in this life. When religion stood entirely upon temper and education, it was thought proper to encourage melancholy, as indeed, mankind never have recourse to superior powers so readily as in that disposition. But as men have now learned to form principles, and to draw consequences, it is necessary to change the batteries, and to make use of such arguments as will endure at least some scrutiny and examination. . . . (Part XI)

PAMPHILUS (Narrator):

After Demea's departure, Cleanthes and Philo continued the conversation in the following manner. . . .

PHILO (skeptic):

"I must confess, . . ." said Philo, "that I am less cautious on the subject of Natural Religion than on any other; both because I know that I can never, on that head, corrupt the principles of any man of common sense, and because no one, I am confident, in whose eyes I appear a man of common sense, will ever mistake my intentions. . . ."

CLEANTHES (Christian reconciler of faith and reason with emphasis on experience):

"I shall further add," said Cleanthes, . . . "that one great advantage of the principle of theism, is, that it is the only system of cosmogony which can be rendered intelligible and complete, and yet can throughout preserve a strong analogy to what we every day see and experience in the world. The comparison of the universe to a machine of human contrivance, is so obvious and natural, and is justified by so many instances of order and design in nature, that it must immediately strike all unprejudiced apprehensions, and procure universal approbation. Whoever attempts to weaken this theory, cannot pretend to succeed by establishing in its place any other that is precise and determinate; it is sufficient for him if he starts doubts and difficulties, and by remote and abstract views of things, reaches that suspense of judgment, which is here the utmost boundary of his wishes. But, besides that this state of mind is in itself unsatisfactory, it can never be steadily maintained against such striking appearances as continually engage us into the religious hypothesis. A false, absurd system, human nature, from the force of prejudice, is capable of adhering to with obstinacy and perseverance; but no system at all, in opposition to a theory supported by strong and obvious reason, by natural propensity, and by early education, I think it absolutely impossible to maintain or defend...."

PHILO (skeptic):

"All men of sound reason are disgusted with verbal disputes, which abound so much in philosophical and theological inquiries; and it is found, that the only remedy for this abuse must arise from clear definitions, from the precision of those ideas which enter into any argument, and from the strict and uniform use of those terms which are employed. But there is a species of controversy, which, from the very nature of language and of human ideas, is involved in perpetual ambiguity, and can never, by any precaution or any definitions, be able to reach a reasonable certainty or precision. These are the controversies concerning the degrees of any quality or circumstance. Men may argue to all eternity, whether Hannibal be a great, or a very great, or a superlatively great man, what degree of beauty Cleopatra possessed. . . . That the dispute concerning theism is of this nature, and consequently is merely verbal, or perhaps, if possible, still more incurably ambiguous, will appear upon the slightest inquiry. I ask the theist, if he does not allow, that there is a great and immeasurable, because incomprehensible difference between the human and the divine mind; the more pious he is, the more readily will he assent to the affirmative, and the more will he be disposed to magnify the difference; he will even assert, that the difference is of a nature which cannot be too much magnified. I next turn to the atheist, . . . and . . . ask him, if it be not probable, that the principle which first arranged, and still maintains order in this universe, bears not also some remote inconceivable analogy to the other operations of nature, and, among the rest, to the economy of human mind and thought. However reluctant, he must give his assent. Where then, cry I to both these antagonists, is the subject of your dispute? The theist allows that the original intelligence is very different from human reason; the atheist allows, that the original principle of order bears some remote analogy to it. Will you quarrel, Gentlemen, about the degrees, and enter into a controversy, which admits not of any precise meaning, nor consequently of any determination? If you should be so obstinate, I should not be surprised to find you insensibly change sides; while the theist, on the one hand, exaggerates the dissimilarity between the Supreme Being, and frail, imperfect, variable, fleeting, and mortal creatures; and the atheist, on the other, magnifies the analogy among all the operations of nature, in every period, every situation, and every position. Consider then, where the real point of controversy lies; and if you cannot lay aside your disputes, endeavor, at least, to cure yourselves of your animosity. . . .

"These, Cleanthes, are my unfeigned sentiments on this subject; and these sentiments, you know, I have ever cherished and maintained. But in proportion to my veneration for true religion, is my abhorrence of vulgar superstitions; and I indulge a peculiar pleasure, I confess, in pushing such principles, sometimes into absurdity, sometimes into impiety. And you are sensible, that all bigots, notwithstanding their great aversion to the latter above the former, are commonly equally guilty of both."

CLEANTHES (Christian reconciler of faith and reason with emphasis on experience):

"My inclination," replied Cleanthes, "lies, I own, a contrary way. Religion, however corrupted, is still better than no religion at all. The doctrine of a future state is so strong and necessary a security to morals, that we never ought to abandon or neglect it. For if finite and temporary rewards and punishments have so great an effect, as we daily find; how much greater must be expected from such as are infinite and eternal?"

PHILO (skeptic):

"How happens it then," said Philo, "if vulgar superstition be so salutary to society, that all history abounds so much with accounts of its pernicious consequences on public affairs? Factions, civil wars, persecutions, subversions of government, oppression, slavery—these are the dismal consequences which always attend its prevalence over the minds of men. If the religious spirit be ever mentioned in any historical narration, we are sure to meet afterwards with a detail of the miseries which attend it. And no period of time can be happier or more prosperous, than those in which it is never regarded or heard of."

CLEANTHES (Christian reconciler of faith and reason with emphasis on experience):

"The reason of this observation," replied Cleanthes, "is obvious. The proper office of religion is to regulate the heart of men, humanize their conduct, infuse the spirit of temperance, order, and obedience; and as its operation is silent, and only enforces the motives of morality and justice, it is in danger of being overlooked, and confounded with these other motives. When it distinguishes itself, and acts as a separate principle over men, it has departed from its proper sphere, and has become only a cover to faction and ambition."

PHILO (skeptic):

"And so will all religion," said Philo, "except the philosophical and rational kind. [In proposing a salutary effect of religion on conduct], . . . consider, I beseech you, the attachment which we have to present things, and the little concern which we discover for objects so remote and uncertain. When divines are declaiming against the common behavior and conduct of the world, they always represent this principle as the strongest imaginable (which indeed it is), and describe almost all human kind as lying under the influence of it, and sunk into the deepest lethargy and unconcern about their religious interests. Yet these same divines, when they refute their speculative antagonists, suppose the motives of religion to be so powerful, that, without them, it were impossible for civil society to subsist, nor are they ashamed of so palpable a contradiction. It is certain, from experience, that the smallest grain of natural honesty and benevolence has more effect on men's conduct, than the most pompous views suggested by theological theories and systems. . . .

". . . This is well understood in the world; and none but fools ever repose less trust in a man, because they hear, that from study and philosophy, he has entertained some speculative doubts with regard to theological subjects. And when we have to do with a man, who makes a great profession of religion and devotion, has this any other effect upon several, who pass for prudent, than to put them on their guard, lest they be cheated and deceived by him? . . .

". . . Even though superstition or enthusiasm should not put itself in direct opposition to morality; the very diverting of the attention, the raising up a new and frivolous species of merit, the preposterous distribution which it makes of praise and blame, must have the most pernicious consequences, and weaken extremely men's attachment to the natural motives of justice and humanity. . . .

"The bad effects of such habits, even in common life, are easily imagined, but, where the interests of religion are concerned, no morality can be forcible enough to bind the enthusiastic zealot. The sacredness of the cause sanctifies every measure which can be made use of to promote it.

"The steady attention alone to so important an interest as that of eternal salvation, is apt to extinguish the benevolent affections, and beget a narrow, contracted selfishness. And when such a temper is encouraged, it easily eludes all the general precepts of charity and benevolence.

"Thus, the motives of vulgar superstition have no great influence on general conduct, nor is their operation favorable to morality, in the instances where they predominate.

"Is there any maxim in politics more certain and infallible, than that both the number and authority of priests should be confined within very narrow limits, and that the civil magistrate ought, forever, to keep his fasces and axes from such dangerous hands? . . .

"True religion, I allow, has no such pernicious consequences; but we must treat of religion, as it has commonly been found in the world. . . ."

CLEANTHES (Christian reconciler of faith and reason with emphasis on experience):

"Take care, Philo," replied Cleanthes, "take care: push not matters too far, allow not your zeal against false religion to undermine your veneration for the true. Forfeit not this principle—the chief, the only great comfort in life, and our principal support amidst all the attacks of adverse fortune. The most agreeable reflection, which it is possible for human imagination to suggest, is that of genuine theism, which represents us as the workmanship of a Being perfectly good, wise, and powerful; who created us for happiness; and who, having implanted in us immeasurable desires of good, will prolong our existence to all eternity, and will transfer us into an infinite variety of scenes, in order to satisfy those desires, and render our felicity complete and durable. . . . The happiest lot which we can imagine, is that of being under his guardianship and protection."

PHILO (skeptic):

"These appearances," said Philo, "are most engaging and alluring. . . . But . . . with regard to the greater part of mankind, the appearances are deceitful, and that the terrors of religion commonly prevail above its comforts. . . .

"It is true, both fear and hope enter into religion because both these passions, at different times, agitate the human mind, and each of them forms a species of divinity suitable to itself. But when a man is in a cheerful disposition, he is fit for business, or company, or entertainment of any kind; and he naturally applies himself to these, and thinks not of religion. When melancholy and dejected, he has nothing to do but brood upon the terrors of the invisible world, and to plunge himself still deeper in affliction. It may indeed happen, that after he has, in this manner, engraved the religious opinions deep into his thought and imagination, there may arrive a change of health or circumstances, which may restore his good humor, and raising cheerful prospects of futurity, make him run into the other extreme of joy and triumph. But still it must be acknowledged, that, as terror is the primary principle of religion, it is the passion which always predominates in it, and admits but of short intervals of pleasure.

"Not to mention, that these fits of excessive, enthusiastic joy, by exhausting the spirits, always prepare the way for equal fits of superstitious terror and dejection, nor is there any state of mind so happy as the calm and equable. But this state it is impossible to support, where a man thinks that he lies in such profound darkness and uncertainty, between an eternity of happiness and an eternity of misery. No wonder that such an opinion disjoints the ordinary frame of the mind, and throws it into the utmost confusion. And though that opinion is seldom so steady in its operation as to influence all the actions; yet it is apt to make a considerable breach in the temper, and to produce that gloom and melancholy so remarkable in all devout people.

"It is contrary to common sense to entertain apprehensions or terrors upon account of any opinion whatsoever, or to imagine that we run any risk hereafter, by the freest use of our reason. Such a sentiment implies both an absurdity and an inconsistency. It is an absurdity to believe that the Deity has human passions, and one of the lowest of human passions, a restless appetite for applause. It is an inconsistency to believe, that, since the Deity has this human passion, he has not others also, and, in particular, a disregard to the opinions of creatures so much inferior.

"'*To know God*,' says Seneca, '*is* [*in itself*] *to worship him*.' All other worship is indeed absurd, superstitious, and even impious. It degrades him to the low condition of mankind, who are delighted with entreaty, solicitation, presents, and flattery. Yet is this impiety the smallest of which superstition is guilty. Commonly, it depresses the Deity far below the condition of mankind, and represents him as a capricious Demon, who exercises his power without reason and without humanity! . . ." (Part XII)

Part Two

Morals

Introduction

Although Hume was a determined enemy of religion in any form, and especially Christianity, he recognized that this left a gap in morals. If God or revealed religion was not to be the source of our morals, what was to take its place?

Could logic take its place? Could clear reasoning from a self-evident (*a priori*) premise to conclusion and then to corollary of the conclusion and then onward from there show us the right way to think about our lives and social relations with other human beings? Hume thought not.

Logic had its place, but only as a tool to help us order the practical lessons taught us by experience. We learn from experience what is both useful and agreeable, and no moral system makes sense if not useful and agreeable. Moreover experience teaches us that what is useful and agreeable in the long run is often of much greater consequence than what seems useful or agreeable at the moment, which is a supreme lesson.

All of this is of the greatest importance, but Hume adds a critical caveat. Even experience has a limited application. Only emotion, which Hume called sentiment, could prompt us to want to act on the wisdom to be gained from experience. We must want to be wise; indeed we must want to be happy. Not everyone actually makes this choice. Ultimately, therefore, morals are based on emotion.

This last point has led to great misunderstanding, as we shall shortly see. Hume does not mean that morals are all about emotion. He does not mean that they do not also include reason and experience as essential pillars. He certainly does not mean that our moral choices are without empirical or logical content, more like the barking of dogs than the considered judgments of human beings. He simply means that emotion gives us the energy and will to make the choices we make, and it is well for us to draw as much wisdom as we can from experience and even logic in making those choices.

It is, however, best to let Hume speak for himself in these matters. Here are a few thoughts of this remarkably kind, gentle, and humane enemy of religion on the proper way to go about developing our morals:

1. ... A considerable part of [philosophy] ...
   arise[s] either from the fruitless efforts of

human vanity, which would penetrate into subjects utterly inaccessible to the understanding, or from the craft of popular superstitions which, being unable to defend themselves on fair ground, raise these entangling brambles to cover and protect their weakness.... (*An Enquiry Concerning Human Understanding*, Section I, 6)

2. ... It seems to me, that the only objects [provable beyond doubt] ... are quantity and number....

All other enquiries of men regard only matter of fact and existence; and these are evidently incapable of ... [absolute proof]....

[Experience] ... is the foundation of moral reasoning...

[But] morals ... are not so properly objects of the understanding as of taste and sentiment. Beauty, whether moral or natural, is felt, more properly than perceived....

When we run over libraries, persuaded of these principles, what havoc must we make? If we take in our hand any volume; of divinity or school metaphysics, for instance; let us ask, *Does it contain any abstract reasoning concerning quantity or number?* No. *Does it contain any experimental reasoning concerning matter of fact and existence?* No. Commit it then to the flames: for it can contain nothing but sophistry and illusion. (Ibid., Section XII, Part III)

3. If we can depend upon any principle which we learn from philosophy, this, I think, may be considered as certain and undoubted, that there is nothing, in itself, valuable or despicable, desirable or hateful, beautiful or deformed; but that these attributes arise from the particular constitution and fabric of human sentiment and affection.... ("The Skeptic")

4. Some men are possessed of great strength of mind; and even when they pursue *external* objects, are not much affected by a disappointment, but renew their application and industry with the greatest cheerfulness. Nothing contributes more to happiness than such a turn of mind.

... The happiest disposition of mind is the *virtuous*; or, in other words, that which leads to action and employment, renders us sensible to the social passions, steels the heart against the assaults of fortune, reduces the affections to a just moderation, makes our own thoughts an entertainment to us, and inclines us rather to the pleasures of society and conversation than to those of the senses. . . .

Habit is another powerful means of reforming the mind, and implanting in it good dispositions and inclinations. . . .

. . . Though virtue be undoubtedly the best choice, when it is attainable, yet such is the disorder and confusion of man's affairs, that no perfect or regular distribution of happiness and misery is ever in this life to be expected. . . . (Ibid.)

5. None of . . . [us] can go beyond experience, or establish any principles which are not founded on that authority. Moral philosophy has, indeed, this peculiar disadvantage, which is not found in natural, that in collecting its experiments, it cannot make them purposely, with premeditation, and after such a manner as to satisfy itself concerning every particular difficulty which may arise. . . . We must therefore glean up our experiments in this science from

a cautious observation of human life, and take them as they appear in the common course of the world, by men's behavior in company, in affairs, and in their pleasures. . . . (*A Treatise of Human Nature*, Introduction)

6. Morality consists not in any [logical] relations . . . ; but if examined, will prove with equal certainty, that it consists not in any matter of [indisputable] fact, which can be discovered by the understanding. . . .

When you pronounce any action or character to be vicious, you mean nothing, but that from the constitution of your nature you have a feeling or sentiment of blame from the contemplation of it. . . .

I cannot forbear adding to these reasonings an observation, which may, perhaps, be found of some importance. In every system of morality, which I have hitherto met with, I have always remarked, that the author proceeds for some time in the ordinary way of reasoning . . . , [making] observations concerning human affairs; when of a sudden I am surprised to find, that instead of the usual copulations of propositions, is, and is not, I meet with no proposition that is not connected with an ought, or an ought not. This change is imperceptible; but is, however, of the last consequence. For as this ought, or ought not, expresses some new relation or affirmation, it is necessary that it should be observed and explained; and at the same time that a reason should be given, for what seems altogether inconceivable, how this new relation can be a deduction from others, which are entirely different from it. But as authors do not commonly use this precaution, I shall presume to recommend it to the readers; and am persuaded, that this small attention would subvert all the vulgar systems of morality, and let us see, that the distinction of vice and virtue is not founded merely on the relations of objects, nor is perceived by reason. (Ibid., Book III, Part I, Section I)

Note: We have already observed that the preceding argument, often summarized as "no ought from an is," may easily be misinterpreted. It does not mean that there is no relationship between the facts we think we glean from observation or personal experience and our value judgments. The latter are not just a witless expression of emotion; Hume makes it clear that he draws conclusions from his personal experience that heavily influence his moral judgments. In his *An Enquiry Concerning the Principles of Morals*, Section I, published only three years after *An Enquiry Concerning Human Understanding*, he also states that mankind should "reject every system of ethics, however subtle or ingenious, which is not founded on fact and observation."

So what then does Hume mean when he says that we should be careful about drawing an ought from an is, a value judgment from what we believe to be a fact, based on observation and experience? In the first place, we are being warned that what we learn from experience depends on individual circumstances. It will not be exactly the same for everybody, even people of the same age. In the second place, the results of our actions are never "pure and unmixed." ("Of the Rise and Progress in the Arts and Sciences") In the third place, even if circumstances and outcomes were not so variable, knowledge gained from observation and experience would never give us absolutely certain knowledge, only probabilities.

Importantly, we also have to want to learn from the "facts" of experience, and want to make our lives better by doing so, or experience will be of no use to us. This desire to improve our lives does not itself come from either logic or experience. It must come from some other source within ourselves. It may be characterized as almost instinctive, built into us, but many people choose to act self-destructively, so it is clearly also a choice.

Can such imperfect knowledge gained from observation and experience, and put to use by our will, actually help us? Hume says yes. Moreover, he argues that such imperfect knowledge is much more valuable than what he characterizes as the spurious and misleading knowledge provided by religion and other systems not based on observation and experience. Hume's further comments will help clarify all this.

> 7. There are ... particulars in our natural temper, and in our outward circumstances, which are very incommodious. ... Among the former, we may justly esteem our selfishness to be the most considerable. ... In the original frame of our mind, our strongest attention is confined to ourselves; our next is extended to our relations and acquaintance; and it is only the weakest which reaches to strangers and indifferent persons. ...
>
> The remedy . . . is not derived from nature, but from artifice. ... It is certain, that no affection of the human mind has both a sufficient force, and a proper direction to counterbalance the love of gain, and render men fit members of society, by

making them abstain from the possessions of others. . . . There is no passion, therefore, capable of controlling the interested affection, but the very affection itself, by an alteration of its direction. Now this alteration must necessarily take place upon the least reflection; since it is evident, that the passion is much better satisfied by its restraint, than by its liberty, and that in preserving society, we make much greater advances in . . . acquiring possessions, than in the solitary and forlorn condition, which must follow upon violence and a universal license. . . . (*A Treatise of Human Nature*, Section II)

. . . Whatever restraint[s] . . . society . . . may impose on the passions of men, they are the real offspring of those passions, and are only a more artful and more refined way of satisfying them. . . . (Ibid., Section VI)

. . . There is no quality in human nature, which causes more fatal errors in our conduct, than that which leads us to prefer whatever is present to the distant and remote, and makes us desire objects more according to their situation than their intrinsic value. . . . This is the reason why men so often act in contradiction to their known interest; and in particular why they prefer any trivial advantage, that is present, to the maintenance of order in society, which so much depends on the observance of justice. The consequence is . . . that . . . violations of equity must become very frequent in society, and the commerce of men, by that means, be rendered very dangerous and uncertain. . . . [This in turn explains] . . . the origin of civil government and society. . . . (Ibid., Section VII)

. . . The common rule [of government in civil society] requires submission; and it is only in cases of grievous tyranny and oppression, that the exception can take place. . . . (Ibid., Section X)

8. . . . We shall endeavor to follow a very simple method . . . in collecting and arranging the estimable or blamable qualities of men. . . . We shall begin our enquiry on this head by the consideration of the social virtues, Benevolence and Justice. . . . (*An Enquiry Concerning the Principles of Morals*, Section I)

... May it not ... [be] concluded, that the utility, resulting from the social virtues, forms, at least, a *part* of their merit, and is one source of that approbation and regard so universally paid to them? ...

In [this instance and in] general, what praise is implied in the simple epithet *useful*! What reproach in the contrary!

In all determinations of morality, this circumstance of public utility is ever principally in view; and wherever disputes arise, either in philosophy or common life, concerning the bounds of duty, the question cannot, by any means, be decided with greater certainty, than by ascertaining, on any side, the true interests of mankind. ...

[Experience teaches what is useful, which may take time and thought.] ... Giving alms to common beggars is naturally praised; because it seems to carry relief to the distressed and indigent; but when we observe the encouragement thence arising to idleness and debauchery, we regard that species of charity rather as a weakness than a virtue. ...

Liberality in princes is regarded as a mark of beneficence, but when it occurs, that the homely bread of the honest and industrious is often thereby converted into delicious cakes for the idle and the prodigal, we soon retract our heedless praises.... (Ibid., Section II, Part II)

Note: Hume's view on alms to street beggars and public welfare continues to be disputed, which illustrates his principal that knowledge derived from observation and experience will always be imperfect and uncertain.

... It seems so natural a thought to ascribe to their utility the praise, which we bestow on the social virtues, that one would expect to meet with this principle everywhere in moral writers, as the chief foundation of their reasoning and enquiry. In common life, we may observe, that the circumstance of utility is always appealed to; nor is it supposed, that a greater eulogy can be given to any man, than to display his usefulness to the public, and enumerate the services, which he has performed to mankind and society.... (Ibid., Section V, Part I) What need we seek for abstruse and remote systems, when there occurs one so obvious and natural?... (Ibid., Section V, Part II)

[Beside the social virtues, there are many others such as] . . . *discretion, caution, enterprise, industry, assiduity, frugality, economy, good-sense, prudence, discernment,* . . . *temperance, sobriety, patience, constancy, perseverance, forethought, considerateness,* . . . *order,* . . . *presence of mind, quickness of conception,* . . . *[and] facility of expression* . . . which tend only to the utility of their possessor, without any reference to us, or to the community, [but yet] are esteemed and valued. . . . (Ibid., Section VI)

. . . Cheerfulness carries great merit with it, and naturally conciliates the goodwill of mankind. No quality, indeed, more readily communicates itself to all around; because no one has a greater propensity to display itself, in jovial talk and pleasant entertainment. The flame spreads through the whole circle; and the most sullen and morose are often caught by it. . . .

From this influence of cheerfulness, both to communicate itself and to engage approbation, we may perceive that there is another set of mental qualities, which, without any utility or any tendency to farther good, either of the community or of the possessor, diffuse a satisfaction on the beholders, and procure friendship and regard. Their immediate sensation, to the person possessed of them, is agreeable. . . .

In all polite nations and ages, a relish for pleasure, if accompanied with temperance and decency, is esteemed a considerable merit, even in the greatest men; and becomes still more requisite in those of inferior rank and character. . . . (Ibid., Section VII)

It may justly appear surprising that any man in so late an age, should find it requisite to prove, by elaborate reasoning, that Personal Merit consists altogether in the possession of mental qualities, *useful* or *agreeable* to the *person himself* or to *others*. . . . And as every quality which is useful or agreeable to ourselves or others is, in common life, allowed to be a part of personal merit; so no other will ever be received, where men judge of things by their natural, unprejudiced reason, without the delusive glosses of superstition and false religion.

Celibacy, fasting, penance, mortification, self-denial, humility, silence, solitude, and the whole train of monkish virtues; for what reason are they everywhere rejected by men of sense, but because they serve to no manner of purpose; neither advance a man's fortune in the world, nor render him a more valuable member of society; neither qualify him for the entertainment of company, nor increase his power of self-enjoyment? We observe, on the contrary, that they cross all these desirable ends; stupefy the understanding and harden the heart, obscure the fancy and sour the temper. We justly, therefore, transfer them to the opposite column, and place them in the catalog of vices; nor has any super-stition force sufficient among men of the world, to pervert entirely these natural sentiments. A gloomy, hair-brained enthusiast, after his death, may have a place in the calendar; but will scarcely ever be admitted, when alive, into intimacy and society, except by those who are as delirious and dismal as himself.

It seems a happiness in the present theory, that it enters not into that vulgar dispute concerning the *degrees* of benevolence or self-love, which prevail in human nature. . . . It is sufficient for our present purpose, if it be allowed, what surely, without the greatest absurdity cannot be disputed, that there is some benevolence, however small, infused into our bosom; some spark of friendship for humankind; some particle of the dove kneaded into our frame, along with the elements of the wolf and serpent. . . .

What wonder then, that moral sentiments are found of such influence in life; though springing from principles, which may appear, at first sight, somewhat small and delicate? But these principles, we must remark, are social and universal; they form, in a manner, the *party* of humankind against vice or disorder, its common enemy. . . . Other passions, though perhaps originally stronger, yet being selfish and private, are often overpowered by its force, and yield the dominion of our breast to those social and public principles. . . .

It must . . . be allowed that every quality of the mind, which is *useful* or *agreeable* to the *person himself* or to *others*, communicates a pleasure to the spectator, engages his esteem, and is admitted under the honorable denomination of virtue or merit. . . . Who can dispute that a mind, which supports a perpetual serenity and cheerfulness, a noble dignity and undaunted spirit, a tender affection and goodwill to all around; as it has more enjoyment within itself, is also a more animating and rejoicing spectacle, than if dejected with melancholy, tormented with anxiety, irritated with rage, or sunk into the most abject baseness and degeneracy? And as to the qualities, immediately *agreeable* to *others*, they speak sufficiently for themselves; and he must be unhappy, indeed, either in his own temper, or in his situation and company, who has never perceived the charms of a facetious wit or flowing affability, of a delicate modesty or decent genteelness of address and manner. . . . (Ibid., Section IX, Conclusion, Part I)

. . . What philosophical truths can be more advantageous to society, than those here delivered, which represent virtue in all her genuine and most engaging charms, and makes us approach her with ease, familiarity, and affection? The dismal dress falls off, with which many divines, and some philosophers, have covered her; and nothing appears but gentleness, humanity, beneficence, affability; nay, even at proper intervals, play, frolic, and gaiety. She talks not of useless austerities and rigors, suffering and self-denial. She declares that her sole purpose is to make her votaries and all mankind, during every instant of their existence, if possible, cheerful and happy; nor does she ever willingly part with any pleasure but in hopes of ample compensation in some other period of their lives. The sole trouble which she demands, is that of just calculation, and a steady preference of the greater happiness. And if any austere pretenders approach her, enemies to joy and pleasure, she either rejects them as hypocrites and deceivers; or, if she admit them in her train, they are ranked, however, among the least favored of her votaries.

And, indeed . . . what theory of morals can ever serve any useful purpose, unless it can show, by a particular detail, that all the duties which it recommends, are also the true interest of each individual? The peculiar advantage of the foregoing system seems to be, that it furnishes proper mediums for that purpose. . . .

I must confess that, if a man thinks that this reasoning much requires an answer, it would be a little difficult to find any which will to him appear satisfactory and convincing.... Inward peace of mind, consciousness of integrity, a satisfactory review of our own conduct; these are circumstances, very requisite to happiness, and will be cherished and cultivated by every honest man, who feels the importance of them....

How little is requisite to supply the *necessities* of nature? And in a view to *pleasure*, what comparison between the unbought satisfaction of conversation, society, study, even health and the common beauties of nature, but above all the peaceful reflection on one's own conduct; what comparison, I say, between these and the feverish, empty amusements of luxury and expense? These natural pleasures, indeed, are really without price; both because they are below all price in their attainment, and above it in their enjoyment. (Ibid., Section IX, Part II)

If the foregoing hypothesis be received,... we may ... examine how far either *reason* or *sentiment* enters into all decisions of praise or censure.

One principal foundation of moral praise being supposed to lie in the usefulness of any quality or action, it is evident that *reason* must enter for a considerable share in all decisions of this kind; since nothing but that faculty can instruct us in the tendency of qualities and actions, and point out their beneficial consequences to society and to their possessor. In many cases this is an affair liable to great controversy: doubts may arise; opposite interests may occur; and a preference must be given to one side, from very nice views, and a small overbalance of utility. . . .

But though reason, when fully assisted and improved, be sufficient to instruct us in the pernicious or useful tendency of qualities and actions; it is not alone sufficient to produce any moral blame or approbation. Utility is only a [means] to a certain end; and were the end totally indifferent to us, we should feel the same indifference towards the means. It is requisite a *sentiment* should here display itself, in order to give a preference to the useful above the pernicious tendencies. This *sentiment* can be no other than a feeling for the happiness of [myself and] mankind, and a resentment of their misery; since these are the different ends which virtue and vice have a tendency to promote. Here therefore *reason* instructs us in the several tendencies of actions, and *humanity* makes a distinction in favor of those which are useful and ... [agreeable]. ... (Ibid., Appendix I)

Note: Christians of Hume's day found his work scandalous for many reasons. First, they regarded religion as the only available bulwark against the human propensity for gluttony, sexual misconduct, anarchy, and violence, while Hume argued just the opposite, that virtue provided its own reward and religion just contributed to superstitious fears, fanaticism, and vice. The notion that chastity was a good idea because it was socially useful, not because sexual license was inherently sinful, even for women, was particularly shocking. The publisher of two of Hume's essays, "On Suicide" and "The Immortality of the Soul," both withheld from publication during the author's lifetime, felt constrained in 1783 to protect himself from possible prosecution by denouncing his own publication in a preface. The intent of publication, the preface stated, was "to expose the ... pitiful ... sophistry of the author" and thus reveal "truth's superiority to error."

Not all of the fire directed at Hume came from the pulpit or popular press. Immanuel Kant, often considered the most important Western philosopher, said that he had been awakened from his "metaphysical slumbers" by Hume and set out to refute the idea that logic cannot give us reliable morals or that experience must be our only guide, however imperfect experience may be. Kant's defense of logic and rejection of experience as our moral guide are contained in a companion volume, *The Essence of Kant's Groundwork of the Metaphysics of Morals* (Axios Press, 2012).

—HUNTER LEWIS

An Enquiry Concerning Human Understanding

(1748)

Section I: Of the Different Species of Philosophy

A CONSIDERABLE PART OF metaphysics . . . is not properly a science; but arises either from the fruitless efforts of human vanity, which would penetrate into subjects utterly inaccessible to the understanding, or from the craft of popular superstitions which, being unable to defend themselves on fair ground, raise these entangling brambles to cover and protect their weakness. Chased from the open country, these robbers fly into the forest, and lie in wait to break in upon every unguarded avenue of the mind, and overwhelm it with religious fears and prejudices. The stoutest antagonist, if he remits his watch a moment, is oppressed. . . .

. . . We must . . . cultivate true metaphysics with some care, in order to destroy the false and adulterate. . . . Accurate and just reasoning is the only catholic remedy, fitted for all persons and all dispositions; and is alone able to subvert that abstruse philosophy and metaphysical jargon, which, being mixed up with popular superstition, renders it in a manner impenetrable to careless reasoners, and gives it the air of science and wisdom. . . .

Section II: Of . . . Skeptical Philosophy

Part III

The *imagination* of man is naturally sublime, delighted with whatever is remote and extraordinary, and running, without control, into the most distant parts of space and time in order to avoid the objects, which custom has rendered too familiar to it. A correct *Judgment* observes a contrary method, and avoiding all distant and high enquiries, confines itself to common life, and to such subjects as fall under daily practice and experience; leaving the more sublime topics to the embellishment of poets and orators, or to the arts of priests and politicians.

... Philosophical decisions are nothing but the reflections of common life, methodized and corrected. ...

It seems to me, that the only objects [provable beyond doubt] ... are quantity and number, and that all attempts to extend this more perfect species of knowledge beyond these bounds are mere sophistry and illusion. ...

That *the square of the hypotenuse is equal to the squares of the other two sides*, cannot be known, let the terms be ever so exactly defined, without a train of reasoning and enquiry. But to convince us of this proposition, *that where there is no property, there can be no injustice*, it is only necessary to define the terms, and explain injustice to be a violation of property. This proposition is, indeed, nothing but a [question of] ... definition. It is the same case with all those pretended syllogistical reasonings, which may be found in every other branch of learning, except the sciences of quantity and number. ... [The latter] may safely, I think, be pronounced the only proper objects of knowledge and demonstration.

All other enquiries of men regard only matter of fact and existence; and these are evidently incapable of demonstration. Whatever *is* may *not be*. No negation of a fact can involve a contradiction. The non-existence of any being, without exception, is as clear and distinct an idea as its existence. ... That the cube root of 64 is equal to the half of 10, is a false proposition, and can never be distinctly conceived. But that Caesar, or the angel Gabriel, or any being never existed, may be a false proposition, but still is perfectly conceivable, and implies no contradiction.

The existence, therefore, of any being can only be proved by arguments from its cause or its effect; and these arguments are founded entirely on experience. If we reason *a priori*, anything may appear able to produce anything. The falling of a pebble may, for aught we know, extinguish the sun; or the wish of a man control the planets in their orbits. It is only experience, which teaches us the nature and bounds of cause and effect, and enables us to infer the existence of one object from that of another. Such is the foundation of moral reasoning, which forms the greater part of human knowledge, and is the source of all human action and behavior. . . .

Morals and criticism are not so properly objects of the understanding as of taste and sentiment. Beauty, whether moral or natural, is felt, more properly than perceived. Or if we reason concerning it, and endeavor to fix its standard, we regard a new fact, to wit, the general tastes of mankind, or some such fact, which may be the object of reasoning and enquiry.

When we run over libraries, persuaded of these principles, what havoc must we make? If we take in our hand any volume; of divinity or school metaphysics, for instance; let us ask, *Does it contain any abstract reasoning concerning quantity or number?* No. *Does it contain any experimental reasoning concerning matter of fact and existence?* No. Commit it then to the flames: for it can contain nothing but sophistry and illusion.

A Treatise of Human Nature

(1738)

Introduction

THERE IS NOTHING which is not the subject of debate, and in which men of learning are not of contrary opinions. . . . No man needs ever despair of gaining proselytes to the most extravagant hypothesis, who has art enough to represent it in any favorable colors. The victory is not gained by the men at arms, who manage the pike and the sword; but by the trumpeters, drummers, and musicians of the army.

And as the science of man is the only solid foundation for the other sciences, so the only solid foundation we can give to this science itself must be laid on experience and observation. . . . [which in turn requires] toleration and of liberty. . . .

None of... [us] can go beyond experience, or establish any principles which are not founded on that authority. Moral philosophy has, indeed, this peculiar disadvantage, which is not found in natural, that in collecting its experiments, it cannot make them purposely, with premeditation, and after such a manner as to satisfy itself concerning every particular difficulty which may arise. ... We must therefore glean up our experiments in this science from a cautious observation of human life, and take them as they appear in the common course of the world, by men's behavior in company, in affairs, and in their pleasures. Where experiments of this kind are judiciously collected and compared, we may hope to establish on them a science which will not be inferior in certainty, and will be much superior in utility to any other of human comprehension.

Book III: Of Morals

Part I: Of Virtue and Vice in General

Section I: Moral Distinctions Not Derived from Reason

Morality is a subject that interests us above all others: We fancy the peace of society to be at stake in every decision concerning it. ...

Those who affirm that virtue is nothing but a conformity to reason; that there are eternal fitnesses and unfitnesses of things, which are the same to every rational being that considers them; that the immutable measures of right and wrong impose an obligation, not only on human creatures, but also on the Deity himself: All these systems concur in the opinion, that morality, like truth, is discerned merely by ideas, and by their juxtaposition and comparison. . . . [But] morals excite passions, and produce or prevent actions. Reason of itself is utterly impotent in this particular. The rules of morality therefore, are not conclusions of our reason. . . .

Actions may be laudable or blamable; but they cannot be reasonable: Laudable or blamable, therefore, are not the same with reasonable or unreasonable. The merit and demerit of actions frequently contradict, and sometimes control our natural propensities. But reason has no such influence. Moral distinctions, therefore, are not the offspring of reason. Reason is wholly inactive, and can never be the source of so active a principle as conscience, or a sense of morals. . . .

There has been an opinion very industriously propagated by certain philosophers, that morality is susceptible of demonstration; and though no one has ever been able to advance a single step in those demonstrations; yet it is taken for granted, that this science may be brought to an equal certainty with geometry or algebra. [Even if this could be achieved] . . . it is one thing to know virtue, and another to conform the will to it. . . .

Morality consists not in any [logical] relations . . . ; but if examined, will prove with equal certainty, that it consists not in any matter of fact, which can be discovered by the understanding. . . .

When you pronounce any action or character to be vicious, you mean nothing, but that from the constitution of your nature you have a feeling or sentiment of blame from the contemplation of it. Vice and virtue, therefore, may be compared to sounds, colors, heat and cold, which, according to modern philosophy, are not qualities in objects, but perceptions in the mind. . . .

I cannot forbear adding to these reasonings an observation, which may, perhaps, be found of some importance. In every system of morality, which I have hitherto met with, I have always remarked, that the author proceeds for some time in the ordinary way of reasoning, and establishes the being of a God, or makes observations concerning human affairs; when of a sudden I am surprised to find, that instead of the usual copulations of propositions, is, and is not, I meet with no proposition that is not connected with an ought, or an ought not. This change is imperceptible; but is, however, of the last consequence. For as this ought, or ought not, expresses some new relation or affirmation, it is necessary that it should be observed and explained; and at the same time that a reason should be given, for what seems altogether inconceivable, how this new relation can be a deduction from others, which are entirely different from it. But as authors do not commonly use this precaution, I shall presume to recommend it to the readers; and am persuaded, that this small attention would subvert all the vulgar systems of morality, and let us see, that the distinction of vice and virtue is not founded merely on the relations of objects, nor is perceived by reason.

Section II: Moral Distinctions Derived from a Moral Sense

Thus the course of the argument leads us to conclude, that since vice and virtue are not discoverable merely by reason, or the comparison of ideas, it must be by means of some impression or sentiment they occasion, that we are able to mark the difference betwixt them. . . . Morality, therefore, is more properly felt than judged of; though this feeling or sentiment is commonly so soft and gentle, that we are apt to confound it with an idea. . . .

All morality depends upon our sentiments; and when any action, or quality of the mind, pleases us after a certain manner, we say it is virtuous; and when the neglect, or nonperformance of it, displeases us after a like manner, we say that we lie under an obligation to perform it.

. . . Every moment's experience must convince us of this. There is no spectacle so fair and beautiful as a noble and generous action; nor any which gives us more abhorrence than one that is cruel and treacherous. No enjoyment equals the satisfaction we receive from the company of those we love and esteem; as the greatest of all punishments is to be obliged to pass our lives with those we hate or condemn. . . .

An action, or sentiment, or character is virtuous or vicious; why? Because its view causes a pleasure or uneasiness of a particular kind. . . . It is evident, that under the term pleasure, we comprehend sensations, which are very different from each other. . . . A good composition of music and a bottle of good wine equally produce pleasure; and what is more, their goodness is determined merely by the pleasure. But shall we say upon that account, that the wine is harmonious, or the music of a good flavor? In like manner an inanimate object, and the character or sentiments of any person may, both of them, give satisfaction; but as the satisfaction is different, this keeps our sentiments concerning them from being confounded, and makes us ascribe virtue to the one, and not to the other.

Nor is every sentiment of pleasure or pain, which arises from characters and actions, of that peculiar kind, which makes us praise or condemn. The good qualities of an enemy are hurtful to us; but may still command our esteem and respect. . . .

Meanwhile it may not be amiss to observe . . . that nothing can be more unphilosophical than those systems, which assert, that virtue is the same with what is natural, and vice with what is unnatural. For in the first sense of the word, Nature, as opposed to miracles, both vice and virtue are equally natural; and in the second sense, as opposed to what is unusual, perhaps virtue will be found to be the most unnatural. At least it must be owned, that heroic virtue, being as unusual, is as little natural as the most brutal barbarity. . . .

Part II: Of Justice and Injustice

Section I: Justice, Whether a Natural or Artificial Virtue?

It is evident, that when we praise any actions, we regard only the motives that produced them, and consider the actions as signs or indications of certain principles in the mind and temper. The external performance has no merit. We must look within to find the moral quality. This we cannot do directly; and therefore fix our attention on actions, as on external signs. But these actions are still considered as signs; and the ultimate object of our praise and approbation is the motive, that produced them. . . .

From this . . . it may be established as an undoubted maxim, *that no action can be virtuous, or morally good, unless there be in human nature some motive to produce it, distinct from the sense of its morality.* . . .

It is requisite, then, to find some motive to acts of justice and honesty, distinct from our regard to the honesty; and in this lies the great difficulty. For should we say, that a concern for our private interest or reputation is the legitimate motive to all honest actions; it would follow, that wherever that concern ceases, honesty can no longer have a place.

In . . . addition, it may be affirmed, that there is no such passion in human minds, as the love of mankind, merely as such, independent of personal qualities, of services, or of relation to ourselves. It is true, there is no human, and indeed no sensible, creature, whose happiness or misery does not, in some measure, affect us when brought near to us, and represented in lively colors: But this proceeds merely from sympathy, and is no proof of such a universal affection to mankind, since this concern extends itself beyond our own species.

If public benevolence, therefore, or a regard to the interests of mankind, cannot be the original motive to justice, much less can private benevolence, or a regard to the interests of the party concerned, be this motive. For what if he be my enemy, and has given me just cause to hate him? What if he be a vicious man, and deserves the hatred of all mankind? What if he be a miser, and can make no use of what I would deprive him of? What if he be a profligate debauchee, and would rather receive harm than benefit from large possessions? What if I be in necessity, and have urgent motives to acquire something to my family?

In all these cases, the original motive to justice would fail; and consequently the justice itself, and along with it all property, right, and obligation. . . .

Section II: Of the Origin of Justice and Property

There are . . . particulars in our natural temper, and in our outward circumstances, which are very incommodious. . . . Among the former, we may justly esteem our selfishness to be the most considerable. I am sensible, that generally speaking, the representations of this quality have been carried much too far; and that the descriptions, which certain philosophers delight so much to form of mankind in this particular, are as wide of nature as any accounts of monsters, which we meet with in fables and romances. So far from thinking, that men have no affection for anything beyond themselves, I am of opinion, that though it be rare to meet with one, who loves any single person better than himself; yet it is as rare to meet with one, in whom all the kind affections, taken together, do not overbalance all the selfish. Consult common experience. Do you not see, that though the whole expense of the family be generally under the direction of the master of it, yet there are few that do not bestow the largest part of their fortunes on the pleasures of their wives, and the education of their children, reserving the smallest portion for their own proper use and entertainment. . . .

Even so . . . it appears, that in the original frame of our mind, our strongest attention is confined to ourselves; our next is extended to our relations and acquaintance; and it is only the weakest which reaches to strangers and indifferent persons. . . .

The remedy . . . is not derived from nature, but from artifice. . . . I observe, that it will be for my interest to leave another in the possession of his goods, provided he will act in the same manner with regard to me. He is sensible of a like interest in the regulation of his conduct. When this common sense of interest is mutually expressed, and is known to both, it produces a suitable resolution and behavior. . . . Two men, who pull the oars of a boat, do it by an agreement or convention, though they have never given promises to each other. . . . It is . . . on the expectation of this, that our moderation and abstinence are founded. In like manner are languages gradually established by human conventions without any promise. In like manner do gold and silver become the common measures of exchange, and are esteemed sufficient payment for what is of a hundred times their value.

After this convention, concerning abstinence from the possessions of others, is entered into, and everyone has acquired a stability in his possessions, there immediately arise the ideas of justice and injustice; as also those of property, right, and obligation. The latter are altogether unintelligible without first understanding the former. . . .

It is certain, that no affection of the human mind has both a sufficient force, and a proper direction to counterbalance the love of gain, and render men fit members of society, by making them abstain from the possessions of others. Benevolence to strangers is too weak for this purpose; and as to the other passions, they rather inflame this avidity, when we observe, that the larger our possessions are, the more ability we have of gratifying all our appetites. There is no passion, therefore, capable of controlling the interested affection, but the very affection itself, by an alteration of its direction. Now this alteration must necessarily take place upon the least reflection; since it is evident, that the passion is much better satisfied by its restraint, than by its liberty, and that in preserving society, we make much greater advances in . . . acquiring possessions, than in the solitary and forlorn condition, which must follow upon violence and a universal license. The question, therefore, concerning the wickedness or goodness of human nature, enters not in the least into that other question concerning the origin of society; nor is there anything to be considered but the degrees of men's sagacity or folly. For whether the passion of self-interest be esteemed vicious or virtuous, it is all a case; since itself alone restrains it: So that if it be virtuous, men become social by their virtue; if vicious, their vice has the same effect. . . .

Nor need we have recourse to the fictions of poets to learn this; but beside the reason of the thing, may discover the same truth by common experience and observation. . . . When there is such a plenty of anything as satisfies all the desires of men; . . . the distinction of property is entirely lost, and everything remains in common. This we may observe with regard to air and water, though the most valuable of all external objects; and may easily conclude, that if men were supplied with everything in the same abundance, or if everyone had the same affection and tender regard for everyone as for himself; justice and injustice would be equally unknown among mankind.

Here then is a proposition, which, I think, may be regarded as certain, that it is only from the selfishness and confined generosity of men, along with the scanty provision nature has made for his wants, that justice derives its origin. . . .

. . . Though in our own actions we may frequently lose sight of that interest, which we have in maintaining order, and may follow a lesser and more present interest, we never fail to observe the prejudice we receive, either mediately or immediately, from . . . being unjust to . . . others. . . .

As public praise and blame increase our esteem for justice; so private education and instruction contribute to the same effect. For as parents easily observe, that a man is the more useful, both to himself and others, the greater degree of probity and honor he is endowed with; and that those principles have greater force, when custom and education assist interest and reflection.

What farther contributes to increase their solidity, is the interest of our reputation, after the opinion, that a merit or demerit attends justice or injustice, is once firmly established among mankind. There is nothing, which touches us more nearly than our reputation, and nothing on which our reputation more depends than our conduct, with relation to the property of others. . . .

Section V: Of the Obligation of Promises

. . . [We learn] that we can better satisfy our appetites in an oblique and artificial manner, than by their headlong and impetuous motion. Hence I learn to do a service to another, without bearing him any real kindness; because I foresee, that he will return my service, in expectation of another of the same kind, and in order to maintain the same correspondence of good offices with me or with others. And accordingly, after I have served him, and he is in possession of the advantage arising from my action, he is induced to perform his part, as foreseeing the consequences of his refusal.

But though this self-interested commerce of man begins to take place, and to predominate in society, it does not entirely abolish the more generous and noble intercourse of friendship and good offices. I may still do services to such persons as I love, and am more particularly acquainted with, without any prospect of advantage; and they may make me a return in the same manner, without any view but that of recompensing my past services. In order, therefore, to distinguish those two different sorts of commerce, the interested and the disinterested, there is a certain form of words invented for the former, by which we bind ourselves to the performance of any action. This form of words constitutes what we call a promise, which is the sanction of the interested commerce of mankind. When a man says he promises anything, he in effect expresses a resolution of performing it; and along with that, by making use of this form of words, subjects himself to the penalty of never being trusted again in case of failure. . . .

There needs but a very little practice of the world, to make us perceive all the . . . consequences and advantages of a system of mutual promises. The shortest experience of society discovers them to every mortal; and when each individual perceives the same sense of interest in all his fellows, he immediately performs his part of any contract, as being assured, that they will not be wanting in theirs. . . . Afterwards a sentiment of morals concurs with interest, and becomes a new obligation upon mankind....

Section VI: Some Farther Reflections concerning Justice and Injustice

We have now run over the three fundamental laws of nature, that of the stability of possession, of its transference by consent, and of the performance of promises. It is on the strict observance of those three laws, that the peace and security of human society entirely depend; nor is there any possibility of establishing a good correspondence among men, where these are neglected. Society is absolutely necessary for the well-being of men; and these are as necessary to the support of society. Whatever restraint they may impose on the passions of men, they are the real offspring of those passions, and are only a more artful and more refined way of satisfying them....

Upon the whole, then, we are to consider the distinction betwixt justice and injustice, as having two different foundations, viz. that of interest, when men observe, that it is impossible to live in society without restraining themselves by certain rules; and that of morality, when this interest is once observed and men receive a pleasure from the view of such actions as tend to the peace of society, and an uneasiness from such as are contrary to it....

Section VII: Of the Origin of Government

... There is no quality in human nature, which causes more fatal errors in our conduct, than that which leads us to prefer whatever is present to the distant and remote, and makes us desire objects more according to their situation than their intrinsic value.... This is the reason why men so often act in contradiction to their known interest; and in particular why they prefer any trivial advantage, that is present, to the maintenance of order in society, which so much depends on the observance of justice. The consequences of every breach of equity seem to lie very remote, and are not able to counter-balance any immediate advantage, that may be reaped from it. They are, however, never the less real for being remote; and as all men are, in some degree, subject to the same weakness, it necessarily happens, that the violations of equity must become very frequent in society, and the commerce of men, by that means, be rendered very dangerous and uncertain. You have the same propensity, that I have, in favor of what is contiguous above what is remote. You are, therefore, naturally carried to commit acts of injustice as well as me. Your example both pushes me forward in this way by imitation, and also affords me a new reason for any breach of equity, by showing me, that I should be the cully of my integrity, if I alone should impose on myself a severe restraint amidst the licentiousness of others.

The . . . difficulty, therefore, is to find out this expedient, by which men cure their natural weakness, and lay themselves under the necessity of observing the laws of justice and equity, notwithstanding their violent propensity to prefer contiguous to remote. . . . Here then is the origin of civil government and society. . . . But this execution of justice, though the principal, is not the only advantage of government. As violent passion hinders men from seeing distinctly the interest they have in an equitable behavior towards others; so it hinders them from seeing that equity itself, and gives them a remarkable partiality in their own favors. This inconvenience is corrected in the same manner as that above-mentioned. The same persons, who execute the laws of justice, will also decide all controversies concerning them; and being indifferent to the greatest part of the society, will decide them more equitably than everyone would in his own case. . . .

But government extends farther its beneficial influence. . . . Two neighbors may agree to drain a meadow, which they possess in common. . . . But it is very difficult, and indeed impossible, that a thousand persons should agree in any such action; it being difficult for them to concert so complicated a design, and still more difficult for them to execute it; while each seeks a pretext to free himself of the trouble and expense, and would lay the whole burden on others. Political society easily remedies both these inconveniences.... Thus bridges are built; harbors opened; ramparts raised; canals formed; fleets equipped; and armies disciplined everywhere, by the care of government....

Section X: Of the Objects of Allegiance

... Though, on some occasions, it may be justifiable, both in sound politics and morality, to resist supreme power, it is certain, that in the ordinary course of human affairs nothing can be more pernicious and criminal; and that besides the convulsions, which always attend revolutions, such a practice tends directly to the subversion of all government, and the causing a universal anarchy and confusion among mankind. As numerous and civilized societies cannot subsist without government, so government is entirely useless without an exact obedience. We ought always to weigh the advantages, which we reap from authority, against the disadvantages; and by this means we shall become more scrupulous of putting in practice the doctrine of resistance. The common rule requires submission; and it is only in cases of grievous tyranny and oppression, that the exception can take place....

In the case of enormous tyranny and oppression, it is lawful to take arms even against supreme power; and that as government is a mere human invention for mutual advantage and security, it no longer imposes any obligation, either natural or moral, when once it ceases to have that tendency. But though this general principle be authorized by common sense, and the practice of all ages, it is certainly impossible for the laws, or even for philosophy, to establish any particular rules, by which we may know when resistance is lawful; and decide all controversies, which may arise on that subject. . . .

Section XI: Of the Laws of Nations

There is a maxim very current in the world, which few politicians are willing to avow, but which has been authorized by the practice of all ages, that there is a system of morals calculated for princes, much more free than that which ought to govern private persons. . . .

Should it be asked, what proportion these two species of morality bear to each other? I would answer, that this is a question, to which we can never give any precise answer. . . .

An Enquiry Concerning the Principles of Morals

(1751)

Section I: Of the General Principles of Morals

IN ORDER . . . to discover the true origin of morals, . . . we shall endeavor to follow a very simple method: We shall analyze . . . [those] mental qualities, which form what, in common life, we call Personal Merit; we shall consider every attribute of the mind, which renders a man an object either of esteem and affection, or of hatred and contempt; every habit or sentiment or faculty, which, if ascribed to any person, implies either praise or blame, and may enter into any panegyric or satire of his character and manners. . . . The very nature of language guides us almost infallibly in forming a judgment of this nature; and as every tongue possesses one set of words which are taken in a good sense, and another in the opposite, the least acquaintance with the idiom suffices, without any reasoning, to direct us in collecting and arranging the estimable or blamable qualities of men. . . .

As this is a question of fact, not of abstract science, we can only expect success, by following the experimental method, and deducing general maxims from a comparison of particular instances. The other scientific method, where a general abstract principle is first established, and is afterwards branched out into a variety of inferences and conclusions, may be more perfect in itself, but suits less the imperfection of human nature, and is a common source of illusion and mistake in this as well as in other subjects. Men are now cured of their passion for hypotheses and systems in natural philosophy, and will hearken to no arguments but those which are derived from experience. It is full time they should attempt a like reformation in all moral disquisitions; and reject every system of ethics, however subtle or ingenious, which is not founded on fact and observation.

We shall begin our enquiry on this head by the consideration of the social virtues, Benevolence and Justice.

The explication of them will probably give us an opening by which the others may be accounted for.

Section II: Of Benevolence

Part I

It may be esteemed, perhaps, a superfluous task to prove, that the benevolent or softer affections are estimable; and wherever they appear, engage the approbation and goodwill of mankind. The epithets *sociable*, *good-natured*, *humane*, *merciful*, *grateful*, *friendly*, *generous*, *beneficent*, or their equivalents, are known in all languages, and universally express the highest merit, which *human nature* is capable of attaining. . . .

Part II

We may observe that, in displaying the praises of any humane, beneficent man, there is one circumstance which never fails to be amply insisted on, namely, the happiness and satisfaction, derived to society from his intercourse and good offices. . . .

If confined to private life, the sphere of his activity is narrower; but his influence is all benign and gentle. If exalted into a higher station, mankind and posterity reap the fruit of his labors. . . .

As these topics of praise never fail to be employed, and with success, where we would inspire esteem for any one; may it not thence be concluded, that the utility, resulting from the social virtues, forms, at least, a *part* of their merit, and is one source of that approbation and regard so universally paid to them? . . .

In [this instance and in] general, what praise is implied in the simple epithet *useful*! What reproach in the contrary!

In all determinations of morality, this circumstance of public utility is ever principally in view; and wherever disputes arise, either in philosophy or common life, concerning the bounds of duty, the question cannot, by any means, be decided with greater certainty, than by ascertaining, on any side, the true interests of mankind. . . .

Giving alms to common beggars is naturally praised; because it seems to carry relief to the distressed and indigent; but when we observe the encouragement thence arising to idleness and debauchery, we regard that species of charity rather as a weakness than a virtue. . . .

Liberality in princes is regarded as a mark of beneficence, but when it occurs, that the homely bread of the honest and industrious is often thereby converted into delicious cakes for the idle and the prodigal, we soon retract our heedless praises. . . .

Upon the whole, then, it seems undeniable, that nothing can bestow more merit on any human creature than the sentiment of benevolence in an eminent degree; and *that a part*, at least, of its merit arises from its tendency to promote the interests of our species, and bestow happiness on human society. . . .

How considerable a *part* of their merit we ought to ascribe to their utility, will better appear from future disquisitions. . . .

Section III: Of Justice

Part I

That Justice is useful to society, and consequently that PART of its merit, at least, must arise from that consideration, it would be a superfluous undertaking to prove. . . .

Part II

If we examine the *particular* laws, by which justice is directed, and property determined; we shall still be presented with the same conclusion. The good of mankind is the only object of all these laws and regulations. Not only is it requisite, for the peace and interest of society, that men's possessions should be separated; but the rules, which we follow, in making the separation, are such as can best be contrived to serve farther the interests of society.

We shall suppose that a creature, possessed of reason, but unacquainted with human nature, deliberates with himself what rules of justice or property would best promote public interest, and establish peace and security among mankind: His most obvious thought would be, to assign the largest possessions to the most extensive virtue, and give everyone the power of doing good, proportioned to his inclination. In a perfect theocracy, where a being, infinitely intelligent, governs by particular volitions, this rule would certainly have place, and might serve to the wisest purposes: But were mankind to execute such a law; so great is the uncertainty of merit, both from its natural obscurity, and from the self-conceit of each individual, that no determinate rule of conduct would ever result from it; and the total dissolution of society must be the immediate consequence. Fanatics may suppose, *that dominion is founded on grace*, and *that saints alone inherit the earth*; but the civil magistrate very justly puts these sublime theorists on the same footing with common robbers, and teaches them by the severest discipline, that a rule, which, in speculation, may seem the most advantageous to society, may yet be found, in practice, totally pernicious and destructive.

That there were *religious* fanatics of this kind in England, during the civil wars. . . . Perhaps the *levelers*, who claimed an equal distribution of property, were a kind of *political* fanatics, which arose from the religious species, and more openly avowed their pretensions; as carrying a more plausible appearance, of being practicable in themselves, as well as useful to human society.

It must, indeed, be confessed, that nature is so liberal to mankind, that, were all her presents equally divided among the species, and improved by art and industry, every individual would enjoy all the necessaries, and even most of the comforts of life; nor would ever be liable to any ills but such as might accidentally arise from the sickly frame and constitution of his body. It must also be confessed, that, wherever we depart from this equality, we rob the poor of more satisfaction than we add to the rich, and that the slight gratification of a frivolous vanity, in one individual, frequently costs more than bread to many families, and even provinces. It may appear withal, that the rule of equality, as it would be highly *useful*, is not altogether *impracticable*; but has taken place, at least in an imperfect degree, in some republics; particularly that of Sparta; where it was attended, it is said, with the most beneficial consequences. Not to mention that the Agrarian laws, so frequently claimed in Rome, and carried into execution in many Greek cities, proceeded, all of them, from a general idea of the utility of this principle.

But historians, and even common sense, may inform us, that, however specious these ideas of *perfect* equality may seem, they are really, at bottom, *impracticable*; and were they not so, would be extremely *pernicious* to human society. Render possessions ever so equal, men's different degrees of art, care, and industry will immediately break that equality. Or if you check these virtues, you reduce society to the most extreme indigence; and instead of preventing want and beggary in a few, render it unavoidable to the whole community. The most rigorous inquisition too is requisite to watch every inequality on its first appearance; and the most severe jurisdiction, to punish and redress it. But besides, that so much authority must soon degenerate into tyranny, and be exerted with great partialities; who can possibly be possessed of it, in such a situation as is here supposed? Perfect equality of possessions, destroying all subordination, weakens extremely the authority of magistracy, and must reduce all power nearly to a level, as well as property.

We may conclude, therefore, that, in order to establish laws for the regulation of property, we must be acquainted with the nature and situation of man; must reject appearances, which may be false, though specious; and must search for those rules, which are, on the whole, most *useful* and *beneficial*. Vulgar sense and slight experience are sufficient for this purpose; where men give not way to too selfish avidity, or too extensive enthusiasm.

Who sees not, for instance, that whatever is produced or improved by a man's art or industry ought, forever, to be secured to him, in order to give encouragement to such *useful* habits and accomplishments?

That the property ought also to descend to children and relations, for the same *useful* purpose? That it may be alienated by consent, in order to beget that commerce and intercourse, which is so *beneficial* to human society? And that all contracts and promises ought carefully to be fulfilled, in order to secure mutual trust and confidence, by which the general *interest* of mankind is so much promoted?

Examine the writers on the laws of nature; and you will always find, that, whatever principles they set out with, they are sure to terminate here at last, and to assign, as the ultimate reason for every rule which they establish, the convenience and necessities of mankind. . . .

The necessity of justice to the support of society is the sole foundation of that virtue; and since no moral excellence is more highly esteemed, we may conclude that this circumstance of usefulness has, in general, the strongest energy, and most entire command over our sentiments. It must, therefore, be the source of a considerable part of the merit ascribed to humanity, benevolence, friendship, public spirit, and other social virtues of that stamp; as it is the sole source of the moral approbation paid to fidelity, justice, veracity, integrity, and those other estimable and useful qualities and principles. . . .

Section IV: Of Political Society

It is evident, that, if government were totally useless, it never could have place, and that the sole foundation of the duty of allegiance is the *advantage*, which it procures to society, by preserving peace and order among mankind.

When a number of political societies are erected, and maintain a great intercourse together, a new set of rules are immediately discovered to be *useful* in that particular situation; and accordingly take place under the title of Laws of Nations. Of this kind are, the sacredness of the person of ambassadors, abstaining from poisoned arms, quarter in war, with others of that kind, which are plainly calculated for the *advantage* of states and kingdoms in their intercourse with each other. . . .

All princes pretend a regard to the rights of other princes; and some, no doubt, without hypocrisy. Alliances and treaties are every day made between independent states, which would only be so much waste of parchment, if they were not found by experience to have *some* influence and authority. . . .

[A principle of utility extends also to family life.] The long and helpless infancy of man requires the combination of parents for the subsistence of their young; and that combination requires the virtue of chastity or fidelity to the marriage bed. Without such a *utility*, it will readily be owned, that such a virtue would never have been thought of.

An infidelity of this nature is much more *pernicious* in *women* than in *men*. Hence the laws of chastity are much stricter over the one sex than over the other. . . .

This principle is also the foundation of most of the laws of good manners; a kind of lesser morality, calculated for the ease of company and conversation. Too much or too little ceremony are both blamed, and everything, which promotes ease, without an indecent familiarity, is useful and laudable.

Constancy in friendships, attachments, and familiarities, is commendable, and is requisite to support trust and good correspondence in society. . . . Even in societies, which are established on principles the most immoral, and the most destructive to the interests of the general society, there are required certain rules, which a species of false honor, as well as private interest, engages the members to observe. Robbers and pirates, it has often been remarked, could not maintain their pernicious confederacy, did they not establish a pew distributive justice among themselves, and recall those laws of equity, which they have violated with the rest of mankind. . . .

Wherever men have any intercourse with each other . . . they cannot even pass each other on the road without rules. Wagoners, coachmen, and postilions have principles, by which they give the way;

and these are chiefly founded on mutual ease and convenience. . . .

To carry the matter farther, we may observe, that it is impossible for men so much as to murder each other without statutes, and maxims, and an idea of justice and honor. War has its laws as well as peace; and even that sportive kind of war, carried on among wrestlers, boxers, cudgel-players, gladiators, is regulated by fixed principles. Common interest and utility beget infallibly a standard of right and wrong among the parties concerned.

Section V: Why Utility Pleases

Part I

It seems so natural a thought to ascribe to their utility the praise, which we bestow on the social virtues, that one would expect to meet with this principle everywhere in moral writers, as the chief foundation of their reasoning and enquiry. In common life, we may observe, that the circumstance of utility is always appealed to; nor is it supposed, that a greater eulogy can be given to any man, than to display his usefulness to the public, and enumerate the services, which he has performed to mankind and society. . . .

But perhaps the difficulty of accounting for these effects of usefulness, or its contrary, has kept philosophers from admitting them into their systems of ethics, and has induced them rather to employ any other principle, in explaining the origin of moral good and evil. But it is no just reason for rejecting any principle, confirmed by experience, that we cannot give a satisfactory account of its origin, nor are able to resolve it into other more general principles....

Usefulness is agreeable, and engages our approbation. This is a matter of fact, confirmed by daily observation. But, *useful*? For what? For somebody's interest, surely. Whose interest then? Not our own only: For our approbation frequently extends farther. It must, therefore, be the interest of those, who are served by the character or action approved of; and these we may conclude, however remote, are not totally indifferent to us. By opening up this principle, we shall discover one great source of moral distinctions.

Part II

Self-love is a principle in human nature of such extensive energy, and the interest of each individual is, in general, so closely connected with that of the community, that those philosophers were excusable, who fancied that all our concern for the public might be resolved into a concern for our own happiness and preservation.... But notwithstanding ... [the] frequent confusion of interests, it is easy to attain what natural philosophers, after Lord Bacon, have affected to call the *experimentum crucis*, or that experiment which points out the right way in any doubt or ambiguity. We have found instances, in which private interest was separate from public; in which it was even contrary: And yet we observed the moral sentiment to continue, notwithstanding this disjunction of interests. And wherever these distinct interests sensibly concurred, we always found a sensible increase of the sentiment, and a more warm affection to virtue, and detestation of vice.

Compelled by these instances, we must renounce the theory, which accounts for every moral sentiment by the principle of self-love. We must adopt a more public affection, and allow, that the interests of society are not, even on their own account, entirely indifferent to us. Usefulness is only a tendency to a certain end; and it is a contradiction in terms, that anything pleases as means to an end, where the end itself in no way affects us. If usefulness, therefore, be a source of moral sentiment, and if this usefulness be not always considered with a reference to self; it follows, that everything, which contributes to the happiness of society, recommends itself directly to our approbation and goodwill. Here is a principle, which accounts, in great part, for the origin of morality: And what need we seek for abstruse and remote systems, when there occurs one so obvious and natural? . . .

Sympathy, we shall allow, is much fainter than our concern for ourselves, and sympathy with persons remote from us much fainter than that with persons near and contiguous; but for this very reason it is necessary for us, in our calm judgments and discourse concerning the characters of men, to neglect all these differences, and render our sentiments more public and social. . . .

. . . If we consider the principles of the human mind, such as they appear to daily experience and observation, we must, *a priori*, conclude it impossible for such a creature as man to be totally indifferent to the well or ill-being of his fellow-creatures. . . . [This seems a] necessary and infallible consequence . . . of the general principles of human nature, as discovered in common life and practice. . . .

It is however hoped, that the progress of this argument will bring a farther confirmation of the present theory, by showing the rise of other sentiments of esteem and regard from the same or like principles.

Section VI: Of Qualities Useful to Ourselves

No quality, it is allowed, is absolutely either blamable or praiseworthy. It is all according to its degree. A due medium, say the Peripatetics, is the characteristic of virtue. But this medium is chiefly determined by utility. A proper celerity, for instance, and dispatch in business, is commendable. When defective, no progress is ever made in the execution of any purpose; when excessive, it engages us in precipitate and ill-concerted measures and enterprises. By such reasonings, we fix the proper and commendable mediocrity in all moral and prudential disquisitions; and never lose view of the advantages, which result from any character or habit. . . .

The best character, indeed, were it not rather too perfect for human nature, is that which is not swayed by temper of any kind; but alternately employs enterprise and caution, as each is useful to the particular purpose intended. Such is the excellence which St. Evremond ascribes to Mareschal Turenne, who displayed in every campaign, as he grew older, more temerity in his military enterprises; and being now, from long experience, perfectly acquainted with every incident in war, he advanced with greater firmness and security, in a road so well known to him. Fabius, says Machiavelli, was cautious; Scipio enterprising: And both succeeded, because the situation of the Roman affairs, during the command of each, was peculiarly adapted to his genius; but both would have failed, had these situations been reversed. He is happy, whose circumstances suit his temper; but he is more excellent, who can suit his temper to any circumstances. . . .

Qualities often derive their merit from complicated sources. *Honesty, fidelity, truth,* are praised for their immediate tendency to promote the interests of society; but after those virtues are once established upon this foundation, they are also considered as advantageous to the person himself, and as the source of that trust and confidence, which can alone give a man any consideration in life. One becomes contemptible, no less than odious, when he forgets the duty, which, in this particular, he owes to himself as well as to society. . . .

All men, it is allowed, are equally desirous of happiness; but few are successful in the pursuit: One considerable cause is the want of strength of mind, which might enable them to resist the temptation of present ease or pleasure, and carry them forward in the search of more distant profit and enjoyment. . . .

A man of a strong and determined temper adheres tenaciously to his general resolutions, and is neither seduced by the allurements of pleasure, nor terrified by the menaces of pain; but keeps still in view those distant pursuits, by which he, at once, ensures his happiness and his honor. . . .

Particular customs and manners alter the usefulness of qualities: they also alter their merit. Particular situations and accidents have, in some degree, the same influence. He will always be more esteemed, who possesses those talents and accomplishments, which suit his station and profession, than he whom fortune has misplaced in the part which she has assigned him. . . .

Of old, the perpetual cant of the *stoics* and *cynics* concerning *virtue*, their magnificent professions and slender performances, bred a disgust in mankind; and Lucian, who, though licentious with regard to pleasure, is yet in other respects a very moral writer, cannot sometimes talk of virtue, so much boasted without betraying symptoms of spleen and irony. But surely this peevish delicacy, whence-ever it arises can never be carried so far as to make us deny the existence of every species of merit, and all distinction of manners and behavior. Besides *discretion, caution, enterprise, industry, assiduity, frugality, economy, good-sense, prudence, discernment*; besides these endowments, I say, whose very names force an avowal of their merit, there are many others, to which the most determined skepticism cannot for a moment refuse the tribute of praise and approbation.

Temperance, sobriety, patience, constancy, perseverance, forethought, considerateness, secrecy, order, insinuation, address, presence of mind, quickness of conception, facility of expression, these, and a thousand more of the same kind, no man will ever deny to be excellences and perfections. . . . [Because] their merit consists in their tendency to serve the person, possessed of them, without any magnificent claim to public and social desert, . . . it is more difficult, in a speculative way, to resolve into self-love the merit which we ascribe to [them, the] selfish virtues. . . , than [is the case with] the social virtues, justice and beneficence. . . . As qualities, which tend only to the utility of their possessor, without any reference to us, or to the community, are yet esteemed and valued; by what theory or system can we account for this sentiment from self-love, or deduce it from that favorite origin? . . .

Section VII: Of Qualities Immediately Agreeable to Ourselves

Whoever has passed an evening with serious melancholy people, and has observed how suddenly the conversation was animated, and what sprightliness diffused itself over the countenance, discourse, and behavior of every one, on the accession of a good-humored, lively companion; such a one will easily allow that cheerfulness carries great merit with it, and naturally conciliates the goodwill of mankind. No quality, indeed, more readily communicates itself to all around; because no one has a greater propensity to display itself, in jovial talk and pleasant entertainment. The flame spreads through the whole circle; and the most sullen and morose are often caught by it. . . .

From this influence of cheerfulness, both to communicate itself and to engage approbation, we may perceive that there is another set of mental qualities, which, without any utility or any tendency to farther good, either of the community or of the possessor, diffuse a satisfaction on the beholders, and procure friendship and regard. Their immediate sensation, to the person possessed of them, is agreeable. . . .

In all polite nations and ages, a relish for pleasure, if accompanied with temperance and decency, is esteemed a considerable merit, even in the greatest men; and becomes still more requisite in those of inferior rank and character. . . .

The utility of courage, both to the public and to the person possessed of it, is an obvious foundation of merit. But to anyone who duly considers of the matter, it will appear that this quality has a peculiar luster, which it derives wholly from itself, and from that noble elevation inseparable from it. . . .

It is indeed observable, that, among all uncultivated nations, who have not as yet had full experience of the advantages attending beneficence, justice, and the social virtues, courage is the predominant excellence; what is most celebrated by poets, recommended by parents and instructors, and admired by the public in general. The ethics of Homer are, in this particular, very different from those of Fénelon, his elegant imitator; and such as were well suited to an age, when one hero, as remarked by Thucydides, could ask another, without offense, whether he were a robber or not. Such also very lately was the system of ethics which prevailed in many barbarous parts of Ireland; if we may credit Spencer, in his judicious account of the state of that kingdom.

Of the same class of virtues with courage is that undisturbed philosophical tranquility, superior to pain, sorrow, anxiety, and each assault of adverse fortune. Conscious of his own virtue, say the philosophers, the sage elevates himself above every accident of life; and securely placed in the temple of wisdom, looks down on inferior mortals engaged in pursuit of honors, riches, reputation, and every frivolous enjoyment. These pretensions, no doubt, when stretched to the utmost, are by far too magnificent for human nature. They carry, however, a grandeur with them, which seizes the spectator, and strikes him with admiration. And the nearer we can approach in practice to this sublime tranquility and indifference (for we must distinguish it from a stupid insensibility), the more secure enjoyment shall we attain within ourselves, and the more greatness of mind shall we discover to the world. . . .

Who admires not Socrates; his perpetual serenity and contentment, amidst the greatest poverty and domestic vexations; his resolute contempt of riches, and his magnanimous care of preserving liberty, while he refused all assistance from his friends and disciples, and avoided even the dependence of an obligation? Epictetus had not so much as a door to his little house or hovel; and therefore, soon lost his iron lamp, the only furniture which he had worth taking. But resolving to disappoint all robbers for the future, he supplied its place with an earthen lamp, of which he very peacefully kept possession ever after.

Among the ancients, the heroes in philosophy, as well as those in war and patriotism, have a grandeur and force of sentiment, which astonishes our narrow souls, and is rashly rejected as extravagant and supernatural. They, in their turn, I allow, would have had equal reason to consider as romantic and incredible, the degree of humanity, clemency, order, tranquility, and other social virtues, to which, in the administration of government, we have attained in modern times, had anyone been then able to have made a fair representation of them. Such is the compensation, which nature, or rather education, has made in the distribution of excellences and virtues, in those different ages.

The merit of benevolence, arising from its utility, and its tendency to promote the good of mankind has been already explained, and is, no doubt, the source of a *considerable* part of that esteem, which is so universally paid to it. But it will also be allowed, that the very softness and tenderness of the sentiment, its engaging endearments, its fond expressions, its delicate attentions, and all that flow of mutual confidence and regard, which enters into a warm attachment of love and friendship: it will be allowed, I say, that these feelings, being delightful in themselves, are necessarily communicated to the spectators, and melt them into the same fondness and delicacy. The tear naturally starts in our eye on the apprehension of a warm sentiment of this nature: our breast heaves, our heart is agitated, and every humane tender principle of our frame is set in motion, and gives us the purest and most satisfactory enjoyment.

Who would live amidst perpetual wrangling, and scolding, and mutual reproaches? The roughness and harshness of these emotions disturb and displease us: we suffer by contagion and sympathy; nor can we remain indifferent spectators, even though certain that no pernicious consequences would ever follow from such angry passions.

As a certain proof that the whole merit of benevolence is not derived from its usefulness, we may observe, that in a kind way of blame, we say, a person is *too good*; when he exceeds his part in society, and carries his attention for others beyond the proper bounds. In like manner, we say, a man is too *high-spirited, too intrepid, too indifferent about fortune*; reproaches, which really, at bottom, imply more esteem than many panegyrics. Being accustomed to rate the merit and demerit of characters chiefly by their useful or pernicious tendencies, we cannot forbear applying the epithet of blame, when we discover a sentiment, which rises to a degree, that is hurtful;

but it may happen, at the same time, that its noble elevation, or its engaging tenderness so seizes the heart, as rather to increase our friendship and concern for the person.

The amours and attachments of Harry the IV of France, during the civil wars of the league, frequently hurt his interest and his cause; but all the young, at least, and amorous, who can sympathize with the tender passions, will allow that this very weakness, for they will readily call it such, chiefly endears that hero, and interests them in his fortunes. . . .

These are some instances of the several species of merit, that are valued for the immediate pleasure which they communicate to the person possessed of them. No views of utility or of future beneficial consequences enter into this sentiment of approbation; yet is it of a kind similar to that other sentiment, which arises from views of a public or private utility. The same social sympathy, we may observe, or fellow-feeling with human happiness or misery, gives rise to both; and this analogy, in all the parts of the present theory, may justly be regarded as a confirmation of it.

Section VIII: Of Qualities Immediately Agreeable to Others

As the mutual shocks, in *society*, and the opposi-tions of interest and self-love have constrained mankind to establish the laws of *justice*, in order to pre-serve the advantages of mutual assistance and protec-tion: In like manner, the eternal contrarieties, in *com-pany*, of men's pride and self-conceit, have introduced the rules of Good Manners or Politeness, in order to facilitate the intercourse of minds, and an undisturbed commerce and conversation. Among well-bred peo-ple, a mutual deference is affected; contempt of oth-ers disguised; authority concealed; attention given to each in his turn; and an easy stream of conversation maintained, without vehemence, without interruption, without eagerness for victory, and without any airs of superiority. These attentions and regards are immedi-ately *agreeable* to others, abstracted from any consider-ation of utility or beneficial tendencies: they conciliate affection, promote esteem, and extremely enhance the merit of the person who regulates his behavior by them.

Many of the forms of breeding are arbitrary and casual; but the thing expressed by them is still the same. A Spaniard goes out of his own house before his guest, to signify that he leaves him master of all. In other countries, the landlord walks out last, as a com-mon mark of deference and regard.

But, in order to render a man perfect *good company*, he must have Wit and Ingenuity as well as good manners. What wit is, it may not be easy to define; but it is easy surely to determine that it is a quality immediately *agreeable* to others, and communicating, on its first appearance, a lively joy and satisfaction to everyone who has any comprehension of it. The most profound metaphysics, indeed, might be employed in explaining the various kinds and species of wit; and many classes of it, which are now received on the sole testimony of taste and sentiment, might, perhaps, be resolved into more general principles. But this is sufficient for our present purpose, that it does affect taste and sentiment, and bestowing an immediate enjoyment, is a sure source of approbation and affection.

In countries where men pass most of their time in conversation, and visits, and assemblies, these *companionable* qualities, so to speak, are of high estimation, and form a chief part of personal merit. In countries where men live a more domestic life, and either are employed in business, or amuse themselves in a narrower circle of acquaintance, the more solid qualities are chiefly regarded. Thus, I have often observed, that, among the French, the first questions with regard to a stranger are, *Is he polite? Has he wit?* In our own country, the chief praise bestowed is always that of a *good-natured, sensible fellow*.

In conversation, the lively spirit of dialogue is *agreeable*, even to those who desire not to have any share in the discourse: hence the teller of long stories, or the pompous declaimer, is very little approved of. But most men desire likewise their turn in the conversation, and regard, with a very evil eye, that *loquacity* which deprives them of a right they are naturally so jealous of.

Custom has established it as a rule, in common societies, that men should not indulge themselves in self-praise, or even speak much of themselves; and it is only among intimate friends or people of very manly behavior, that one is allowed to do himself justice. . . .

He must be a very superficial thinker, who imagines that all instances of mutual deference are to be understood in earnest, and that a man would be more estimable for being ignorant of his own merits and accomplishments. A small bias towards modesty, even in the internal sentiment, is favorably regarded, especially in young people; and a strong bias is required in the outward behavior; but this excludes not a noble pride and spirit, which may openly display itself in its full extent, when one lies under calumny or oppression of any kind. The generous contumacy of Socrates, as Cicero calls it, has been highly celebrated in all ages; and when joined to the usual modesty of his behavior, forms a shining character. . . .

A desire of fame, reputation, or a character with others, is so far from being blamable, that it seems inseparable from virtue, genius, capacity, and a generous or noble disposition. An attention even to trivial matters, in order to please, is also expected and demanded by society; and no one is surprised, if he find a man in company to observe a greater elegance of dress and more pleasant flow of conversation, than when he passes his time at home, and with his own family. Wherein, then, consists Vanity, which is so justly regarded as a fault or imperfection? It seems to consist chiefly in such an intemperate display of our advantages, honors, and accomplishments; in such an importunate and open demand of praise and admiration, as is offensive to others, and encroaches too far on *their* secret vanity and ambition. It is besides a sure symptom of the want of true dignity and elevation of mind, which is so great an ornament in any character. For why that impatient desire of applause; as if you were not justly entitled to it, and might not reasonably expect that it would forever attend you? Why so anxious to inform us of the great company which you have kept; the obliging things which were said to you; the honors, the distinctions which you met with; as if these were not things of course, and what we could readily, of ourselves, have imagined, without being told of them? . . .

Among the other virtues, we may also give Cleanliness a place; since it naturally renders us agreeable to others, and is no inconsiderable source of love and affection. No one will deny, that a negligence in this particular is a fault; and as faults are nothing but smaller vices, and this fault can have no other origin than the uneasy sensation which it excites in others; we may, in this instance, seemingly so trivial, clearly discover the origin of moral distinctions, about which the learned have involved themselves in such mazes of perplexity and error.

But besides all the *agreeable* qualities, the origin of whose beauty we can, in some degree, explain and account for, there still remains something mysterious and inexplicable, which conveys an immediate satisfaction to the spectator, but how, or why, or for what reason, he cannot pretend to determine. There is a manner, a grace, an ease, a genteelness, an I-know-not-what, which some men possess above others, which is very different from external beauty and comeliness, and which, however, catches our affection almost as suddenly and powerfully. And though this *manner* be chiefly talked of in the passion between the sexes, where the concealed magic is easily explained, yet surely much of it prevails in all our estimation of characters, and forms no inconsiderable part of personal merit. This class of accomplishments, therefore, must be trusted entirely to the blind, but sure testimony of taste and sentiment; and must be considered as a part of ethics, left by nature to baffle all the pride of philosophy, and make her sensible of her narrow boundaries and slender acquisitions.

We approve of another, because of his wit, politeness, modesty, decency, or any agreeable quality which he possesses; although he be not of our acquaintance, nor has ever given us any entertainment, by means of these accomplishments. The idea, which we form of their effect on his acquaintance, has an agreeable influence on our imagination, and gives us the sentiment of approbation. This principle enters into all the judgments which we form concerning manners and characters.

Section IX: Conclusion

Part I

It may justly appear surprising that any man in so late an age, should find it requisite to prove, by elaborate reasoning, that Personal Merit consists altogether in the possession of mental qualities, *useful* or *agreeable* to the *person himself* or to *others*. It might be expected that this principle would have occurred even to the first rude, unpracticed enquirers concerning morals, and been received from its own evidence, without any argument or disputation. Whatever is valuable in any kind, so naturally classes itself under the division of *useful* or *agreeable*, the *utile* or the *dulce*, that it is not easy to imagine why we should ever seek further, or consider the question as a matter of nice research or inquiry. . . . It seems a reasonable presumption, that systems and hypotheses have perverted our natural understanding, when a theory, so simple and obvious, could so long have escaped the most elaborate examination.

But however the case may have fared with philosophy, in common life these principles are still implicitly maintained; nor is any other topic of praise or blame ever recurred to, when we employ any panegyric or satire, any applause or censure of human action and behavior. If we observe men, in every intercourse of business or pleasure, in every discourse and conversation, we shall find them nowhere, except the schools, at any loss upon this subject. What so natural, for instance, as the following dialogue? You are very happy, we shall suppose one to say, addressing himself to another, that you have given your daughter to Cleanthes. He is a man of honor and humanity. Everyone, who has any intercourse with him, is sure of *fair* and *kind* treatment. I congratulate you too, says another, on the promising expectations of this son-in-law; whose assiduous application to the study of the laws, whose quick penetration and early knowledge both of men and business, prognosticate the greatest honors and advancement. You surprise me, replies a third, when you talk of Cleanthes as a man of business and application. I met him lately in a circle of the gayest company, and he was the very life and soul of our conversation; so much wit with good manners; so much gallantry without affectation; so much ingenious knowledge so genteelly delivered, I have never before observed in any one. You would admire him still more, says a fourth, if you knew him more familiarly. That cheerfulness, which you might remark in him, is not a sudden flash struck out by company: it runs through the whole tenor of his life, and preserves a perpetual serenity on his countenance, and tranquility in his soul. He has met with severe trials, misfortunes as well as dangers; and by his greatness of mind, was still superior to all of them. The image, gentlemen, which you have here delineated of Cleanthes, cried I, is that of accomplished merit. Each of you has given a stroke of the pencil to his figure; and you have unawares exceeded all the pictures drawn by Gratian or Castiglione. A philosopher might select this character as a model of perfect virtue.

And as every quality which is useful or agreeable to ourselves or others is, in common life, allowed to be a part of personal merit; so no other will ever be received, where men judge of things by their natural, unprejudiced reason, without the delusive glosses of superstition and false religion. Celibacy, fasting, penance, mortification, self-denial, humility, silence, solitude, and the whole train of monkish virtues; for what reason are they everywhere rejected by men of sense, but because they serve to no manner of purpose; neither advance a man's fortune in the world, nor render him a more valuable member of society; neither qualify him for the entertainment of company, nor increase his power of self-enjoyment? We observe, on the contrary, that they cross all these desirable ends; stupefy the understanding and harden the heart, obscure the fancy and sour the temper. We justly, therefore, transfer them to the opposite column, and place them in the catalog of vices; nor has any superstition force sufficient among men of the world, to pervert entirely these natural sentiments. A gloomy, hair-brained enthusiast, after his death, may have a place in the calendar; but will scarcely ever be admitted, when alive, into intimacy and society, except by those who are as delirious and dismal as himself.

It seems a happiness in the present theory, that it enters not into that vulgar dispute concerning the *degrees* of benevolence or self-love, which prevail in human nature; a dispute which is never likely to have any issue, both because men, who have taken part, are not easily convinced, and because the phenomena, which can be produced on either side, are so dispersed, so uncertain, and subject to so many interpretations, that it is scarcely possible accurately to compare them, or draw from them any determinate inference or conclusion. It is sufficient for our present purpose, if it be allowed, what surely, without the greatest absurdity cannot be disputed, that there is some benevolence, however small, infused into our bosom; some spark of friendship for humankind; some particle of the dove kneaded into our frame, along with the elements of the wolf and serpent. Let these generous sentiments be supposed ever so weak; let them be insufficient to move even a hand or finger of our body, they must still direct the determinations of our mind, and where everything else is equal, produce a cool preference of what is useful and serviceable to mankind, above what is pernicious and dangerous. *A moral distinction*, therefore, immediately arises; a general sentiment of blame and approbation; a tendency, however faint, to the objects of the one, and a proportional aversion to those of the other. Nor will those reasoners, who so earnestly maintain the predominant selfishness of humankind, be any wise scandalized at hearing of the weak sentiments of virtue implanted in our nature. . . .

Avarice, ambition, vanity, and all passions vulgarly, though improperly, comprised under the denomination of *self-love*, are here excluded from our theory concerning the origin of morals, not because they are too weak, but because they have not a proper direction for that purpose. The notion of morals implies some sentiment common to all mankind, which recommends the same object to general approbation, and makes every man, or most men, agree in the same opinion or decision concerning it. It also implies some sentiment, so universal and comprehensive as to extend to all mankind, and render the actions and conduct, even of the persons the most remote, an object of applause or censure, according as they agree or disagree with that rule of right which is established. . . .

When a man denominates another his *enemy*, his *rival*, his *antagonist*, his *adversary*, he is understood to speak the language of self-love, and to express sentiments, peculiar to himself, and arising from his particular circumstances and situation. But when he bestows on any man the epithets of *vicious* or *odious* or *depraved*, he then speaks another language, and expresses sentiments, in which he expects all his audience are to concur with him. . . . While the human heart is compounded of the same elements as at present, it will never be wholly indifferent to public good, nor entirely unaffected with the tendency of characters and manners. And though this affection of humanity may not generally be esteemed so strong as vanity or ambition, yet, being common to all men, it can alone be the foundation of morals, or of any general system of blame or praise. One man's ambition is not another's ambition, nor will the same event or object satisfy both; but the humanity of one man is the humanity of every one, and the same object touches this passion in all human creatures. . . .

What wonder then, that moral sentiments are found of such influence in life; though springing from principles, which may appear, at first sight, somewhat small and delicate? But these principles, we must remark, are social and universal; they form, in a manner, the *party* of humankind against vice or disorder, its common enemy. And as the benevolent concern for others is diffused, in a greater or less degree, over all men, and is the same in all, it occurs more frequently in discourse, is cherished by society and conversation, and the blame and approbation, consequent on it, are thereby roused from that lethargy into which they are probably lulled, in solitary and uncultivated nature. Other passions, though perhaps originally stronger, yet being selfish and private, are often overpowered by its force, and yield the dominion of our breast to those social and public principles.

Another spring of our constitution, that brings a great addition of force to moral sentiments, is the love of fame; which rules, with such uncontrolled authority, in all generous minds, and is often the grand object of all their designs and undertakings. By our continual and earnest pursuit of a character, a name, a reputation in the world, we bring our own deportment and conduct frequently in review, and consider how they appear in the eyes of those who approach and regard us. This constant habit of surveying ourselves, as it were, in reflection, keeps alive all the sentiments of right and wrong, and begets, in noble natures, a certain reverence for themselves as well as others, which is the surest guardian of every virtue. The animal conveniences and pleasures sink gradually in their value; while every inward beauty and moral grace is studiously acquired, and the mind is accomplished in every perfection, which can adorn or embellish a rational creature.

It must . . . be allowed that every quality of the mind, which is *useful* or *agreeable* to the *person himself* or to *others*, communicates a pleasure to the spectator, engages his esteem, and is admitted under the honorable denomination of virtue or merit. Are not justice, fidelity, honor, veracity, allegiance, chastity, esteemed solely on account of their tendency to promote the good of society? Is not that tendency inseparable from humanity, benevolence, lenity, generosity, gratitude, moderation, tenderness, friendship, and all the other social virtues? Can it possibly be doubted that industry, discretion, frugality, secrecy, order, perseverance, forethought, judgment, and this whole class of virtues and accomplishments, of which many pages would not contain the catalog; can it be doubted, I say, that the tendency of these qualities to promote the interest and happiness of their possessor, is the sole foundation of their merit? Who can dispute that a mind, which supports a perpetual serenity and cheerfulness, a noble dignity and undaunted spirit, a tender affection and goodwill to all around; as it has more enjoyment within itself, is also a more animating and rejoicing spectacle, than if dejected with melancholy, tormented with anxiety, irritated with rage, or sunk into the most abject baseness and degeneracy? And as to the qualities, immediately *agreeable* to *others*, they speak sufficiently for themselves; and he must be unhappy, indeed, either in his own temper, or in his situation and company, who has never perceived the charms of a facetious wit or flowing affability, of a delicate modesty or decent genteelness of address and manner. . . .

Part II

Having explained the moral *approbation* attending merit or virtue, there remains nothing but briefly to consider our interested *obligation* to it, and to inquire whether every man, who has any regard to his own happiness and welfare, will not best find his account in the practice of every moral duty. If this can be clearly ascertained from the foregoing theory, we shall have the satisfaction to reflect, that we have advanced principles, which not only, it is hoped, will stand the test of reasoning and inquiry, but may contribute to the amendment of men's lives, and their improvement in morality and social virtue. And though the philosophical truth of any proposition by no means depends on its tendency to promote the interests of society; yet a man has but a bad grace, who delivers a theory, however true, which, he must confess, leads to a practice dangerous and pernicious. . . . Truths which are *pernicious* to society, if any such there be, will yield to errors which are salutary and *advantageous*.

But what philosophical truths can be more advantageous to society, than those here delivered, which represent virtue in all her genuine and most engaging charms, and makes us approach her with ease, familiarity, and affection? The dismal dress falls off, with which many divines, and some philosophers, have covered her; and nothing appears but gentleness, humanity, beneficence, affability; nay, even at proper intervals, play, frolic, and gaiety. She talks not of useless austerities and rigors, suffering and self-denial. She declares that her sole purpose is to make her votaries and all mankind, during every instant of their existence, if possible, cheerful and happy; nor does she ever willingly part with any pleasure but in hopes of ample compensation in some other period of their lives. The sole trouble which she demands, is that of just calculation, and a steady preference of the greater happiness. And if any austere pretenders approach her, enemies to joy and pleasure, she either rejects them as hypocrites and deceivers; or, if she admits them in her train, they are ranked, however, among the least favored of her votaries.

And, indeed, to drop all figurative expression, what hopes can we ever have of engaging mankind to a practice which we confess full of austerity and rigor? Or what theory of morals can ever serve any useful purpose, unless it can show, by a particular detail, that all the duties which it recommends, are also the true interest of each individual? The peculiar advantage of the foregoing system seems to be, that it furnishes proper mediums for that purpose.

That the virtues which are immediately *useful* or *agreeable* to the person possessed of them, are desirable in a view to self-interest, it would surely be superfluous to prove. Moralists, indeed, may spare themselves all the pains which they often take in recommending these duties. To what purpose collect arguments to evince that temperance is advantageous, and the excesses of pleasure hurtful, when it appears that these excesses are only denominated such, because they are hurtful; and that, if the unlimited use of strong liquors, for instance, no more impaired health or the faculties of mind and body than the use of air or water, it would not be a whit more vicious or blamable?

It seems equally superfluous to prove, that the *companionable* virtues of good manners and wit, decency and genteelness, are more desirable than the contrary qualities. Vanity alone, without any other consideration, is a sufficient motive to make us wish for the possession of these accomplishments. No man was ever willingly deficient in this particular. All our failures here proceed from bad education, want of capacity, or a perverse and unpliable disposition. Would you have your company coveted, admired, followed; rather than hated, despised, avoided? Can anyone seriously deliberate in the case? As no enjoyment is sincere, without some reference to company and society; so no society can be agreeable, or even tolerable, where a man feels his presence unwelcome, and discovers all around him symptoms of disgust and aversion.

But why, in the greater society or confederacy of mankind, should not the case be the same as in particular clubs and companies? Why is it more doubtful, that the enlarged virtues of humanity, generosity, beneficence, are desirable with a view of happiness and self-interest, than the limited endowments of ingenuity and politeness? . . .

Whatever contradiction may vulgarly be supposed between the *selfish* and *social* sentiments or dispositions, they are really no more opposite than selfish and ambitious, selfish and revengeful, selfish and vain. . . . The goods of fortune are spent in one gratification or another: the miser who accumulates his annual income, and lends it out at interest, has really spent it in the gratification of his avarice. And it would be difficult to show why a man is more a loser by a generous action, than by any other method of expense; since the utmost which he can attain by the most elaborate selfishness, is the indulgence of some affection.

Now if life, without passion, must be altogether insipid and tiresome; let a man suppose that he has full power of modeling his own disposition, and let him deliberate what appetite or desire he would choose for the foundation of his happiness and enjoyment. Every affection, he would observe, when gratified by success, gives a satisfaction proportioned to its force and violence; but besides this advantage, common to all, the immediate feeling of benevolence and friendship, humanity and kindness, is sweet, smooth, tender, and agreeable, independent of all fortune and accidents. These virtues are besides attended with a pleasing consciousness or remembrance, and keep us in humor with ourselves as well as others; while we retain the agreeable reflection of having done our part towards mankind and society. And though all men show a jealousy of our success in the pursuits of avarice and ambition; yet are we almost sure of their goodwill and good wishes, so long as we persevere in the paths of virtue, and employ ourselves in the execution of generous plans and purposes. What other passion is there where we shall find so many advantages united; an agreeable sentiment, a pleasing consciousness, a good reputation? But of these truths, we may observe, men are, of themselves, pretty much convinced; nor are they deficient in their duty to society, because they would not wish to be generous, friendly, and humane; but because they do not feel themselves such.

Treating vice with the greatest candor, and making it all possible concessions, we must acknowledge that there is not, in any instance, the smallest pretext for giving it the preference above virtue, with a view of self-interest; except, perhaps, in the case of justice, where a man, taking things in a certain light, may often seem to be a loser by his integrity. And though it is allowed that, without a regard to property, no society could subsist; yet according to the imperfect way in which human affairs are conducted, a sensible knave, in particular incidents, may think that an act of iniquity or infidelity will make a considerable addition to his fortune, without causing any considerable breach in the social union and confederacy. That *honesty is the best policy*, may be a good general rule, but is liable to many exceptions; and he, it may perhaps be thought, conducts himself with most wisdom, who observes the general rule, and takes advantage of all the exceptions.

I must confess that, if a man thinks that this reasoning much requires an answer, it would be a little difficult to find any which will to him appear satisfactory and convincing. If his heart rebels not against such pernicious maxims, if he feels no reluctance to the thoughts of villainy or baseness, he has indeed lost a considerable motive to virtue; and we may expect that this practice will be answerable to his speculation. But in all ingenuous natures, the antipathy to treachery and roguery is too strong to be counter-balanced by any views of profit or pecuniary advantage. Inward peace of mind, consciousness of integrity, a satisfactory review of our own conduct; these are circumstances, very requisite to happiness, and will be cherished and cultivated by every honest man, who feels the importance of them.

Such a one has, besides, the frequent satisfaction of seeing knaves, with all their pretended cunning and abilities, betrayed by their own maxims; and while they purpose to cheat with moderation and secrecy, a tempting incident occurs, nature is frail, and they give into the snare; whence they can never extricate themselves, without a total loss of reputation, and the forfeiture of all future trust and confidence with mankind.

But were they ever so secret and successful, the honest man, if he has any tincture of philosophy, or even common observation and reflection, will discover that they themselves are, in the end, the greatest dupes, and have sacrificed the invaluable enjoyment of a character, with themselves at least, for the acquisition of worthless toys and gewgaws. How little is requisite to supply the *necessities* of nature? And in a view to *pleasure*, what comparison between the unbought satisfaction of conversation, society, study, even health and the common beauties of nature, but above all the peaceful reflection on one's own conduct; what comparison,

I say, between these and the feverish, empty amusements of luxury and expense? These natural pleasures, indeed, are really without price; both because they are below all price in their attainment, and above it in their enjoyment.

Appendix I: Concerning Moral Sentiment

If the foregoing hypothesis be received, . . . we may . . . examine how far either *reason* or *sentiment* enters into all decisions of praise or censure.

One principal foundation of moral praise being supposed to lie in the usefulness of any quality or action, it is evident that *reason* must enter for a considerable share in all decisions of this kind; since nothing but that faculty can instruct us in the tendency of qualities and actions, and point out their beneficial consequences to society and to their possessor. In many cases this is an affair liable to great controversy: Doubts may arise; opposite interests may occur; and a preference must be given to one side, from very nice views, and a small overbalance of utility. This is particularly remarkable in questions with regard to justice. . . . Were every single instance of justice, like that of benevolence, useful to society; this would be a more simple state of the case, and seldom liable to great controversy. But as single instances of justice are often pernicious in their first and immediate tendency, and as the advantage to society results only from the observance of the general rule, and from the concurrence and combination of several persons in the same equitable conduct; the case here becomes more intricate and involved. The various circumstances of society; the various consequences of any practice; the various interests which may be proposed; these, on many occasions, are doubtful, and subject to great discussion and inquiry. The object of municipal laws is to fix all the questions with regard to justice: the debates of civilians; the reflections of politicians; the precedents of history and public records, are all directed to the same purpose. And a very accurate *reason* or *judgment* is often requisite, to give the true determination, amidst such intricate doubts arising from obscure or opposite utilities.

But though reason, when fully assisted and improved, be sufficient to instruct us in the pernicious or useful tendency of qualities and actions; it is not alone sufficient to produce any moral blame or approbation. Utility is only a tendency to a certain end; and were the end totally indifferent to us, we should feel the same indifference towards the means. It is requisite a *sentiment* should here display itself, in order to give a preference to the useful above the pernicious tendencies. This *sentiment* can be no other than a feeling for the happiness of mankind, and a resentment of their misery; since these are the different ends which virtue and vice have a tendency to promote. Here therefore *reason* instructs us in the several tendencies of actions, and *humanity* makes a distinction in favor of those which are useful and beneficial.

When a man, at any time, deliberates concerning his own conduct (as, whether he had better, in a particular emergence, assist a brother or a benefactor), he must consider these separate relations, with all the circumstances and situations of the persons, in order to determine the superior duty and obligation; and in order to determine the proportion of lines in any triangle, it is necessary to examine the nature of that figure, and the relation which its several parts bear to each other. But notwithstanding this appearing similarity in the two cases, there is, at bottom, an extreme difference between them. A speculative reasoner concerning triangles or circles considers the several known and given relations of the parts of these figures; and thence infers some unknown relation, which is dependent on the former. But in moral deliberations we must be acquainted beforehand with all the objects, and all their relations to each other; and from a comparison of the whole, fix our choice or approbation. No new fact to be ascertained; no new relation to be discovered. All the circumstances of the case are supposed to be laid before us, ere we can fix any sentence of blame or approbation. If any material circumstance be yet unknown or doubtful, we must first employ our inquiry or intellectual faculties to assure us of it; and must suspend for a time all moral decision or sentiment. While we are ignorant whether a man were aggressor or not, how can we determine whether the person who killed him be criminal or innocent? But after every circumstance, every relation is known, the understanding has no further room to operate, nor any object on which it could employ itself. The approbation or blame which then ensues, cannot be the work of the judgment, but of the heart; and is not a speculative proposition or affirmation, but an active feeling or sentiment. In the disquisitions of the understanding, from known circumstances and relations, we infer some new and unknown. In moral decisions, all the circumstances and relations must be previously known; and the mind, from the contemplation of the whole, feels some new impression of affection or disgust, esteem or contempt, approbation or blame.

Hence the great difference between a mistake of *fact* and one of *right*; and hence the reason why the one is commonly criminal and not the other. When Oedipus killed Laius (his father), he was ignorant of the relation, and from circumstances, innocent and involuntary, formed erroneous opinions concerning the action which he committed. But when Nero killed Agrippina (his mother), all the relations between himself and the person, and all the circumstances of the fact, were previously known to him; but the motive of revenge, or fear, or interest, prevailed in his savage heart over the sentiments of duty and humanity. And when we express that detestation against him to which he himself, in a little time, became insensible, it is not that we see any relations, of which he was ignorant; but that, for the rectitude of our disposition, we feel sentiments against which he was hardened from flattery and a long perseverance in the most enormous crimes. In these sentiments then, not in a discovery of relations of any kind, do all moral determinations consist. Before we can pretend to form any decision of this kind, everything must be known and ascertained on the side of the object or action. Nothing remains but to feel, on our part, some sentiment of blame or approbation; whence we pronounce the action criminal or virtuous.

This doctrine will become still more evident, if we compare moral beauty with natural, to which in many particulars it bears so near a resemblance. It is on the proportion, relation, and position of parts, that all natural beauty depends; but it would be absurd thence to infer, that the perception of beauty, like that of truth in geometrical problems, consists wholly in the perception of relations, and was performed entirely by the understanding or intellectual faculties. In all the sciences, our mind from the known relations investigates the unknown. But in all decisions of taste or external beauty, all the relations are beforehand obvious to the eye; and we thence proceed to feel a sentiment of complacency or disgust, according to the nature of the object, and disposition of our organs.

Euclid has fully explained all the qualities of the circle; but has not in any proposition said a word of its beauty. The reason is evident. The beauty is not a quality of the circle. It lies not in any part of the line, whose parts are equally distant from a common center. It is only the effect which that figure produces upon the mind, whose peculiar fabric of structure renders it susceptible of such sentiments. In vain would you look for it in the circle, or seek it, either by your senses or by mathematical reasoning, in all the properties of that figure.

Attend to Palladio and Perrault, while they explain all the parts and proportions of a pillar. They talk of the cornice, and frieze, and base, and entablature, and shaft, and architrave; and give the description and position of each of these members. But should you ask the description and position of its beauty, they would readily reply, that the beauty is not in any of the parts or members of a pillar, but results from the whole, when that complicated figure is presented to an intelligent mind, susceptible to those finer sensations. Till such a spectator appears, there is nothing but a figure of such particular dimensions and proportions; from his sentiments alone arise its elegance and beauty.

Again; attend to Cicero, while he paints the crimes of a Verres or a Catiline. You must acknowledge that the moral turpitude results, in the same manner, from the contemplation of the whole, when presented to a being whose organs have such a particular structure and formation. The orator may paint rage, insolence, barbarity on the one side; meekness, suffering, sorrow, innocence on the other. But if you feel no indignation or compassion arise in you from this complication of circumstances, you would in vain ask him, in what consists the crime or villainy, which he so vehemently exclaims against? At what time, or on what subject it first began to exist? And what has a few months afterwards become of it, when every disposition and thought of all the actors is totally altered or annihilated? No satisfactory answer can be given to any of these questions, upon the abstract hypothesis of morals; and we must at last acknowledge, that the crime or immorality is no particular fact or relation, which can be the object of the understanding, but arises entirely from the sentiment of disapprobation, which, by the structure of human nature, we unavoidably feel on the apprehension of barbarity or treachery.

It appears evident that—the ultimate ends of human actions can never, in any case, be accounted for by reason, but recommend themselves entirely to the sentiments and affections of mankind, without any dependence on the intellectual faculties. Ask a man *why he uses exercise*; he will answer, *because he desires to keep his health*. If you then enquire, *why he desires health*, he will readily reply, *because sickness is painful*. If you push your enquiries farther, and desire a reason *why he hates pain*, it is impossible he can ever give any. This is an ultimate end, and is never referred to any other object.

Perhaps to your second question, *why he desires health*, he may also reply, that *it is necessary for the exercise of his calling*. If you ask, *why he is anxious on that head*, he will answer, *because he desires to get money*. If you demand *Why? It is the instrument of pleasure*, says he. And beyond this it is an absurdity to ask for a reason. It is impossible there can be a progress *in infinitum*; and that one thing can always be a reason why another is desired. Something must be desirable on its own account, and because of its immediate accord or agreement with human sentiment and affection.

Now as virtue is an end, and is desirable on its own account, without fee and reward, merely for the immediate satisfaction which it conveys; it is requisite that there should be some sentiment which it touches, some internal taste or feeling, or whatever you may please to call it, which distinguishes moral good and evil, and which embraces the one and rejects the other.

Thus the distinct boundaries and offices of *reason* and of *taste* are easily ascertained. The former conveys the knowledge of truth and falsehood: the latter gives the sentiment of beauty and deformity, vice and virtue. The one discovers objects as they really stand in nature, without addition and diminution: the other has a productive faculty, and gilding or staining all natural objects with the colors, borrowed from internal sentiment, raises in a manner a new creation. Reason being cool and disengaged, is no motive to action, and directs only the impulse received from appetite or inclination, by showing us the means of attaining happiness or avoiding misery: Taste, as it gives pleasure or pain, and thereby constitutes happiness or misery, becomes a motive to action, and is the first spring or impulse to desire and volition. From circumstances and relations, known or supposed, the former leads us to the discovery of the concealed and unknown: after all circumstances and relations are laid before us, the latter makes us feel from the whole a new sentiment of blame or approbation. The standard of the one, being founded on the nature of things, is eternal and inflexible, even by the will of the Supreme Being: the standard of the other arising from the eternal frame and constitution of animals, is ultimately derived from that Supreme Will, which bestowed on each being its peculiar nature, and arranged the several classes and orders of existence.

Appendix II: Of Self-Love

There is a principle, supposed to prevail among many, which is utterly incompatible with all virtue or moral sentiment; and as it can proceed from nothing but the most depraved disposition, so in its turn it tends still further to encourage that depravity. This principle is, that all *benevolence* is mere hypocrisy, friendship a cheat, public spirit a farce, fidelity a snare to procure trust and confidence; and that while all of us, at bottom, pursue only our private interest, we wear these fair disguises, in order to put others off their guard, and expose them the more to our wiles and machinations. What heart one must be possessed of who possesses such principles, and who feels no internal sentiment that belies so pernicious a theory, it is easy to imagine; and also what degree of affection and benevolence he can bear to a species whom he represents under such odious colors, and supposes so little susceptible of gratitude or any return of affection. Or if we should not ascribe these principles wholly to a corrupted heart, we must at least account for them from the most careless and precipitate examination. Superficial reasoners, indeed, observing many false pretenses among mankind, and feeling, perhaps, no very strong restraint in their own disposition, might draw a general and a hasty conclusion that all is equally corrupted, and that men, different from all other animals, and indeed from all other species of existence, admit of no degrees of good or bad, but are, in every instance, the same creatures under different disguises and appearances.

There is another principle, somewhat resembling the former; which has been much insisted on by philosophers, and has been the foundation of many a system; that, whatever affection one may feel, or imagine he feels for others, no passion is, or can be disinterested; that the most generous friendship, however sincere, is a modification of self-love; and that, even unknown to ourselves, we seek only our own gratification, while we appear the most deeply engaged in schemes for the liberty and happiness of mankind. . . .

But though the question concerning the universal or partial selfishness of man be not so material as is usually imagined to morality and practice, it is certainly of consequence in the speculative science of human nature, and is a proper object of curiosity and enquiry. It may not, therefore, be unsuitable, in this place, to bestow a few [further] reflections upon it.

The most obvious objection to the selfish hypothesis is, that, as it is contrary to common feeling and our most unprejudiced notions, there is required the highest stretch of philosophy to establish so extraordinary a paradox. To the most careless observer there appears to be such dispositions as benevolence and generosity; such affections as love, friendship, compassion, gratitude. These sentiments have their causes, effects, objects, and operations, marked by common language and observation, and plainly distinguished from those of the selfish passions. And as this is the obvious appearance of things, it must be admitted, till some hypothesis be discovered, which by penetrating deeper into human nature, may prove the former affections to be nothing but modifications of the latter. . . .

Animals are found susceptible of kindness, both to their own species and to ours; nor is there, in this case, the least suspicion of disguise or artifice. Shall we account for all *their* sentiments, too, from refined deductions of self-interest? Or if we admit a disinterested benevolence in the inferior species, by what rule of analogy can we refuse it in the superior?

Love between the sexes begets a complacency and goodwill, very distinct from the gratification of an appetite. Tenderness to their offspring, in all sensible beings, is commonly able alone to counter-balance the strongest motives of self-love, and has no manner of dependence on that affection. What interest can a fond mother have in view, who loses her health by assiduous attendance on her sick child, and afterwards languishes and dies of grief, when freed, by its death, from the slavery of that attendance? . . .

These and a thousand other instances are marks of a general benevolence in human nature, where no *real* interest binds us to the object. And how an *imaginary* interest known and avowed for such, can be the origin of any passion or emotion, seems difficult to explain. No satisfactory hypothesis of this kind has yet been discovered. . . .

But farther, if we consider rightly of the matter, we shall find that the hypothesis which allows of a disinterested benevolence, distinct from self-love, has really more *simplicity* in it, and is more conformable to the analogy of nature than that which pretends to resolve all friendship and humanity into this latter principle. There are bodily wants or appetites acknowledged by everyone, which necessarily precede all sensual enjoyment, and carry us directly to seek possession of the object. Thus, hunger and thirst have eating and drinking for their end; and from the gratification of these primary appetites arises a pleasure, which may become the object of another species of desire or inclination that is secondary and interested. In the same manner there are mental passions by which we are impelled immediately to seek particular objects, such as fame or power, or vengeance without any regard to interest; and when these objects are attained a pleasing enjoyment ensues, as the consequence of our indulged affections. Nature must, by the internal frame and constitution of the mind, give an original propensity to fame, ere we can reap any pleasure from that acquisition, or pursue it from motives of self-love, and desire of happiness. If I have no vanity, I take no delight in praise; if I be void of ambition, power gives me no enjoyment; if I be not angry, the punishment of an adversary is totally indifferent to me. In all these cases there is a passion which points immediately to the object, and constitutes it our good or happiness; as there are other secondary passions which afterwards arise, and pursue it as a part of our happiness, when once it is constituted such by our original affections. Were there no appetite of any kind antecedent to self-love, that propensity could scarcely ever exert itself; because we should, in that case, have felt few and slender pains or pleasures, and have little misery or happiness to avoid or to pursue.

Now where is the difficulty in conceiving, that this may likewise be the case with benevolence and friendship, and that, from the original frame of our temper, we may feel a desire of another's happiness or good, which, by means of that affection, becomes our own good, and is afterwards pursued, from the combined motives of benevolence and self-enjoyments? Who sees not that vengeance, from the force alone of passion, may be so eagerly pursued, as to make us knowingly neglect every consideration of ease, interest, or safety; and, like some vindictive animals, infuse our very souls into the wounds we give an enemy; and what a malignant philosophy must it be, that will not allow to humanity and friendship the same privileges which are indisputably granted to the darker passions of enmity and resentment. . . .

Selected Essays

(1742)

The Skeptic

I F WE CAN depend upon any principle which we
learn from philosophy, this, I think, may be considered as certain and undoubted, that there is
nothing, in itself, valuable or despicable, desirable or
hateful, beautiful or deformed; but that these attributes arise from the particular constitution and fabric of human sentiment and affection. What seems
the most delicious food to one animal, appears loathsome to another; what affects the feeling of one with
delight, produces uneasiness in another. This is confessedly the case with regard to all the bodily senses.
But, if we examine the matter more accurately, we
shall find that the same observation holds even where

the mind concurs with the body, and mingles its sentiment with the exterior appetite. . . .

We may push the same observation further, and may conclude that, even when the mind operates alone, and feeling the sentiment of blame or approbation, pronounces one object deformed and odious, another beautiful and amiable; I say that, even in this case, those qualities are not really in the objects, but belong entirely to the sentiment of that mind which blames or praises. . . .

Beauty and worth are merely of a relative nature, and consist in an agreeable sentiment, produced by an object in a particular mind, according to the peculiar structure and constitution of that mind. . . .

If I examine the Ptolemaic and Copernican systems, I endeavor only, by my inquiries, to know the real situation of the planets; that is, in other words, I endeavor to give them, in my conception, the same relations that they bear towards each other in the heavens. To this operation of the mind, therefore, there seems to be always a real, though often an unknown standard, in the nature of things; nor is truth or falsehood variable by the various apprehensions of mankind. Though all the human race should forever conclude that the sun moves, and the earth remains at rest, the sun stirs not an inch from his place for all these reasonings; and such conclusions are eternally false and erroneous.

But the case is not the same with the qualities of *beautiful and deformed, desirable and odious*, as with truth and falsehood. In the former case, the mind is not content with merely surveying its objects, as they stand in themselves: it also feels a sentiment of delight or uneasiness, approbation or blame, consequent to that survey; and this sentiment determines it to affix the epithet *beautiful or deformed, desirable or odious*. ...

But a little reflection suffices to distinguish them. A man may know exactly all the circles and ellipses of the Copernican system, and all the irregular spirals of the Ptolemaic, without perceiving that the former is more beautiful than the latter. Euclid has fully explained every quality of the circle, but has not, in any proposition, said a word of its beauty. The reason is evident. Beauty is not a quality of the circle. It lies not in any part of the line, *whose* parts are all equally distant from a common center. It is only the effect, which that figure produces upon a mind, whose particular fabric or structure renders it susceptible of such sentiments. In vain would you look for it in the circle, or seek it, either by your senses, or by mathematical reasonings, in all the properties of that figure. ...

The inference upon the whole is, that it is not from the value or worth of the object which any person pursues, that we can determine his enjoyment, but merely from the passion with which he pursues it, and the success which he meets with in his pursuit. Objects have absolutely no worth or value in themselves. . . .

To be happy, the *passion* must neither be too violent, nor too remiss. In the first case, the mind is in a perpetual hurry and tumult; in the second, it sinks into a disagreeable indolence and lethargy.

To be happy, the passion must be benign and social, not rough or fierce. The affections of the latter kind are not near so agreeable to the feeling as those of the former. Who will compare rancor and animosity, envy and revenge, to friendship, benignity, clemency, and gratitude?

To be happy, the passion must be cheerful and gay, not gloomy and melancholy. A propensity to hope and joy is real riches; one to fear and sorrow, real poverty. . . .

Though the tempers of men be very different, yet we may safely pronounce in general, that a life of pleasure cannot support itself so long as one of business, but is much more subject to satiety and disgust. The amusements which are the most durable, have all a mixture of application and attention in them; such as gaming and hunting. And in general, business and action fill up all the great vacancies in human life.

But where the temper is the best disposed for any *enjoyment*, the object is often wanting; and in this respect, the passions, which pursue external objects, contribute not so much to happiness as those which rest in ourselves; since we are neither so certain of attaining such objects, nor so secure in possessing them. A passion for learning is preferable, with regard to happiness, to one for riches.

Some men are possessed of great strength of mind; and even when they pursue *external* objects, are not much affected by a disappointment, but renew their application and industry with the greatest cheerfulness. Nothing contributes more to happiness than such a turn of mind.

According to this short and imperfect sketch of human life, the happiest disposition of mind is the *virtuous*; or, in other words, that which leads to action and employment, renders us sensible to the social passions, steels the heart against the assaults of fortune, reduces the affections to a just moderation, makes our own thoughts an entertainment to us, and inclines us rather to the pleasures of society and conversation than to those of the senses. This, in the meantime, must be obvious to the most careless reasoner, that all dispositions of mind are not alike favorable to happiness, and that one passion or humor may be extremely desirable, while another is equally disagreeable. And, indeed, all the difference between the conditions of life depends upon the mind; nor is there any one situation of affairs, in itself, preferable to another. Good and ill, both natural and moral, are entirely relative to human sentiment and affection. No man would ever be unhappy, could he alter his feelings. Proteus-like, he would elude all attacks, by the continual alterations of his shape and form.

But of this resource nature has, in a great measure, deprived us. The fabric and constitution of our mind no more depends on our choice, than that of our body. The generality of men have not even the smallest notion that any alteration in this respect can ever be desirable. As a stream necessarily follows the several inclinations of the ground on which it runs, so are the ignorant and thoughtless part of mankind actuated by their natural propensities. Such are effectually excluded from all pretensions to philosophy, and the *medicine of the mind*, so much boasted. But even upon the wise and thoughtful, nature has a prodigious influence; nor is it always in a man's power, by the utmost art and industry, to correct his temper, and attain that virtuous character to which he aspires. The empire of philosophy extends over a few; and with regard to these, too, her authority is very weak and limited. Men may well be sensible of the value of virtue, and may desire to attain it; but it is not always certain that they will be successful in their wishes.

Whoever considers, without prejudice, the course of human actions, will find, that mankind is almost entirely guided by constitution and temper, and that general maxims have little influence, but so far as they affect our taste or sentiment. If a man has a lively sense of honor and virtue, with moderate passions, his conduct will always be conformable to the rules of morality: or if he departs from them, his return will be easy and expeditious. On the other hand, where one is born of so perverse a frame of mind, of so callous and insensible a disposition, as to have no relish for virtue and humanity, no sympathy with his fellow-creatures, no desire of esteem and applause, such a one must be allowed entirely incurable; nor is there any remedy in philosophy. He reaps no satisfaction but from low and sensual objects, or from the indulgence of malignant passions; he feels no remorse to control his vicious inclinations; he has not even that sense or taste, which is requisite to make him desire a better character. For my part, I know not how I should address myself to such a one, or by what arguments I should endeavor to reform him. Should I tell him of the inward satisfaction which results from laudable and humane actions, and delicate pleasure of disinterested love and friendship, the lasting enjoyments of a good name and an established character, he might still reply, that these were, perhaps, pleasures to such as were susceptible of them; but that, for his part, he finds himself of a quite different turn and disposition. I must repeat it, my philosophy affords no remedy in such a case; nor could I do anything but lament this person's unhappy condition. But then I ask, If any other philosophy can afford a remedy; or if it be possible, by any system, to render all mankind virtuous, however perverse may be their natural frame of mind? Experience will soon convince us of the contrary; and I will venture to affirm, that, perhaps, the chief benefit which results from philosophy, arises in an indirect manner, and proceeds more from its secret insensible influence, than from its immediate application. . . .

Habit is another powerful means of reforming the mind, and implanting in it good dispositions and inclinations. A man, who continues in a course of sobriety and temperance, will hate riot and disorder; if he engages in business or study, indolence will seem a punishment to him; if he constrains himself to practice beneficence and affability, he will soon abhor all instances of pride and violence. Where one is thoroughly convinced that the virtuous course of life is preferable; if he has but resolution enough, for some time, to impose a violence on himself; his reformation needs not be despaired of. The misfortune is, that this conviction and this resolution never can have place, unless a man be, beforehand, tolerably virtuous.

Here then is the chief triumph of art and philosophy: it insensibly refines the temper, and it points out to us those dispositions which we should endeavor to attain, by a constant *bent* of mind, and by repeated *habit*. Beyond this I cannot acknowledge it to have great influence; and I must entertain doubts concerning all those exhortations and consolations, which are in such vogue among speculative reasoners. . . .

A man may as well pretend to cure himself of love, by viewing his mistress through the *artificial* medium of a microscope or prospect, and beholding there the coarseness of her skin, and monstrous disproportion of her features, as hope to excite or moderate any passion by the *artificial* arguments of a Seneca or an Epictetus. The remembrance of the natural aspect and situation of the object will, in both cases, still recur upon him. The reflections of philosophy are too subtle and distant to take place in common life, or eradicate any affection. The air is too fine to breathe in, where it is above the winds and clouds of the atmosphere.

Another defect of those refined reflections which philosophy suggests to us, is, that commonly they cannot diminish or extinguish our vicious passions, without diminishing or extinguishing such as are virtuous, and rendering the mind totally indifferent and inactive. They are, for the most part, general, and are applicable to all our affections. In vain do we hope to direct their influence only to one side. If by incessant study and meditation we have rendered them intimate and present to us, they will operate throughout, and spread a universal insensibility over the mind. When we destroy the nerves, we extinguish the sense of pleasure, together with that of pain, in the human body.

It will be easy, by one glance of the eye, to find one or other of these defects in most of those philosophical reflections, so much celebrated both in ancient and modern times. *Let not the injuries or violence of men,* say the philosophers, *ever discompose you by anger or hatred. Would you be angry at the ape for its malice, or the tiger for its ferocity?* This reflection leads us into a bad opinion of human nature, and must extinguish the social affections. It tends also to prevent all remorse for a man's own crimes, when he considers that vice is as natural to mankind as the particular instincts to brute creatures.

All ills arise from the order of the universe, which is absolutely perfect. Would you wish to disturb so divine an order for the sake of your own particular interest? What if the ills I suffer arise from malice or oppression? *But the vices and imperfections of men are also comprehended in the order of the universe.*

> If plagues and earthquakes break not
>   heaven's design,
> Why then a Borgia or a Catiline?
> Let this be allowed, and my own vices will
>   also be a part of the same order. . . .

There are two considerations chiefly to be met within books of philosophy. . . . When we reflect on the shortness and uncertainty of life, how despicable seem all our pursuits of happiness! And even if we would extend our concern beyond our own life, how frivolous appear our most enlarged and most generous projects, when we consider the incessant changes and revolutions of human affairs, by which laws and learning, books and governments, are hurried away by time, as by a rapid stream, and are lost in the immense ocean of matter! Such a reflection certainly tends to mortify all our passions: but does it not thereby counterwork the artifice of nature, who has happily deceived us into an opinion, that human life is of some importance? And may not such a reflection be employed with success by voluptuous reasoners, in order to lead us from the paths of action and virtue, into the flowery fields of indolence and pleasure? . . .

The *second* philosophical consideration, which may often have an influence on the affections, is derived from a comparison of our own condition with the condition of others. This comparison we are continually making even in common life; but the misfortune is, that we are rather apt to compare our situation with that of our superiors, than with that of our inferiors. A philosopher corrects this natural infirmity, by turning his view to the other side, in order to render himself easy in the situation to which fortune has confined him. There are few people who are not susceptible of some consolation from this reflection, though, to a very good-natured man, the view of human miseries should rather produce sorrow than comfort, and add, to his lamentations for his own misfortunes, a deep compassion for those of others. Such is the imperfection, even of the best of these philosophical topics of consolation.

I shall conclude this subject with observing, that, though virtue be undoubtedly the best choice, when it is attainable, yet such is the disorder and confusion of man's affairs, that no perfect or regular distribution of happiness and misery is ever in this life to be expected. Not only the goods of fortune, and the endowments of the body (both of which are important), not only these advantages, I say, are unequally divided between the virtuous and vicious, but even the mind itself partakes, in some degree, of this disorder; and the most worthy character, by the very constitution of the passions, enjoys not always the highest felicity. . . .

With regard to the economy of the mind, we may observe, that all vice is indeed pernicious; yet the disturbance or pain is not measured out by nature with exact proportion to the degrees of vice; nor is the man of highest virtue, even abstracting from external accidents, always the most happy. A gloomy and melancholy disposition is certainly, *to our sentiments*, a vice or imperfection; but as it may be accompanied with great sense of honor and great integrity, it may be found in very worthy characters, though it is sufficient alone to embitter life, and render the person affected with it completely miserable. On the other hand, a selfish villain may possess a spring and alacrity of temper, a certain *gaiety of heart*, which is indeed a good quality, but which is rewarded much beyond its merit, and when attended with good fortune, will compensate for the uneasiness and remorse arising from all the other vices. . . .

In a word, human life is more governed by fortune than by reason; is to be regarded more as a dull pastime than a serious occupation; and is more influenced by particular humor, than by general principles. Shall we engage ourselves in it with passion and anxiety? It is not worthy of so much concern. Shall we be indifferent about what happens? We lose all the pleasure of the game by our phlegm and carelessness. While we are reasoning concerning life, life is gone; and death, though *perhaps* they receive him differently, yet treats alike the fool and the philosopher. To reduce life to exact rule and method is commonly a painful, oft a fruitless occupation; and is it not also a proof, that we overvalue the prize for which we contend? Even to reason so carefully concerning it, and to fix with accuracy its just idea, would be overvaluing it, were it not that, to some tempers, this occupation is one of the most amusing in which life could possibly be employed.

Of the Standard of Taste

Whoever recommends any moral virtues, really does no more than is implied in the terms themselves. That people who invented the word *charity*, and used it in a good sense, inculcated more clearly, and much more efficaciously, the precept, *be charitable*, than any pretended legislator or prophet, who should insert such a *maxim* in his writings. Of all expressions, those which, together with their other meaning, imply a degree either of blame or approbation, are the least liable to be perverted or mistaken.

It is natural for us to seek a *Standard of Taste*; a rule by which the various sentiments of men may be reconciled; at least a decision afforded confirming one sentiment, and condemning another.

There is a species of philosophy, which cuts off all hopes of success in such an attempt, and represents the impossibility of ever attaining any standard of taste. The difference, it is said, is very wide between judgment and sentiment. All sentiment is right; because sentiment has a reference to nothing beyond itself, and is always real, wherever a man is conscious of it. But all determinations of the understanding are not right; because they have a reference to something beyond themselves, to wit, real matter of fact; and are not always conformable to that standard. Among a thousand different opinions which different men may entertain of the same subject, there is one, and but one, that is just and true; and the only difficulty is to fix and ascertain it. On the contrary, a thousand different sentiments, excited by the same object, are all right; because no sentiment represents what is really in the object. It only marks a certain conformity or relation between the object and the organs or faculties of the mind; and if that conformity did not really exist, the sentiment could never possibly have being. Beauty is no quality in things themselves: it exists merely in the mind which contemplates them; and each mind perceives a different beauty. One person may even perceive deformity, where another is sensible of beauty; and every individual ought to acquiesce in his own sentiment, without pretending to regulate those of others. To seek the real beauty, or real deformity, is as fruitless an inquiry, as to pretend to ascertain the real sweet or real bitter. According to the disposition of the organs, the same object may be both sweet and bitter; and the proverb has justly determined it to be fruitless to dispute concerning tastes. It is very natural, and even quite necessary, to extend this axiom to mental, as well as bodily taste; and thus common sense, which is so often at variance with philosophy, especially with the skeptical kind, is found, in one instance at least, to agree in pronouncing the same decision.

But though this axiom, by passing into a proverb, seems to have attained the sanction of common sense; there is certainly a species of common sense, which opposes it, at least serves to modify and restrain it. Whoever would assert an equality of genius and elegance between Ogilby and Milton, or Bunyan and Addison, would be thought to defend no less an extravagance, than if he had maintained a mole-hill to be as high as Teneriffe, or a pond as extensive as the ocean. Though there may be found persons, who give the preference to the former authors; no one pays attention to such a taste; and we pronounce, without scruple, the sentiment of these pretended critics to be absurd and ridiculous. The principle of the natural equality of tastes is then totally forgotten, and while we admit it on some occasions, where the objects seem near an equality, it appears an extravagant paradox, or rather a palpable absurdity, where objects so disproportioned are compared together.

It is evident that none of the rules of composition are fixed by reasonings *a priori*, or can be esteemed abstract conclusions of the understanding, from comparing those habitudes and relations of ideas, which are eternal and immutable. Their foundation is the same with that of all the practical sciences, experience; nor are they anything but general observations, concerning what has been universally found to please. . . .

But though all the general rules of art are founded only on experience, and on the observation of the common sentiments of human nature, we must not imagine, that, on every occasion, the feelings of men will be conformable to these rules. Those finer emotions of the mind are of a very tender and delicate nature, and require the concurrence of many favorable circumstances to make them play with facility and exactness, according to their general and established principles. . . .

Though it be certain that beauty and deformity, more than sweet and bitter, are not qualities in objects, but belong entirely to the sentiment, internal or external, it must be allowed, that there are certain qualities in objects which are fitted by nature to produce those particular feelings. Now, as these qualities may be found in a small degree, or may be mixed and confounded with each other, it often happens that the taste is not affected with such minute qualities, or is not able to distinguish all the particular flavors, amidst the disorder in which they are presented. Where the organs are so fine as to allow nothing to escape them, and at the same time so exact as to perceive every ingredient in the composition, this we call delicacy of taste, whether we employ these terms in the literal or metaphorical sense. . . . It is acknowledged to be the perfection of every sense or faculty, to perceive with exactness its most minute objects, and allow nothing to escape its notice and observation. The smaller the objects are which become sensible to the eye, the finer is that organ, and the more elaborate its make and composition. A good palate is not tried by strong flavors, but by a mixture of small ingredients, where we are still sensible of each part, notwithstanding its minuteness and its confusion with the rest. In like manner, a quick and acute perception of beauty and deformity must be the perfection of our mental taste; nor can a man be satisfied with himself while he suspects that any excellence or blemish in a discourse has passed him unobserved. In this case, the perfection of the man, and the perfection of the sense of feeling, are found to be united. A very delicate palate, on many occasions, may be a great inconvenience both to a man himself and to his friends. But a delicate taste of wit or beauty must always be a desirable quality, because it is the source of all the finest and most innocent enjoyments of which human nature is susceptible. In this decision the sentiments of all mankind are agreed. Wherever you can ascertain a delicacy of taste, it is sure to meet with approbation and the best way of ascertaining it is, to appeal to those models and principles which have been established by the uniform consent and experience of nations and ages. . . .

A man who has had no opportunity of comparing the different kinds of beauty, is . . . totally unqualified to pronounce an opinion with regard to any object presented to him. By comparison alone we fix the epithets of praise or blame, and learn how to assign the due degree of each. . . .

But to enable a critic the more fully to execute this undertaking, he must preserve his mind free from all *prejudice*, and allow nothing to enter into his consideration, but the very object which is submitted to his examination. . . .

But where are such critics to be found? By what marks are they to be known? How distinguish them from pretenders? These questions are embarrassing; and seem to throw us back into the same uncertainty from which, during the course of this essay, we have endeavored to extricate ourselves.

But if we consider the matter aright, these are questions of fact, not of sentiment. Whether any particular person be endowed with good sense and a delicate imagination, free from prejudice, may often be the subject of dispute, and be liable to great discussion and inquiry: but that such a character is valuable and estimable, will be agreed in by all mankind. Where these doubts occur, men can do no more than in other disputable questions which are submitted to the understanding: they must produce the best arguments that their invention suggests to them; they must acknowledge a true and decisive standard to exist somewhere, to wit, real existence and matter of fact; and they must have indulgence to such as differ from them in their appeals to this standard. It is sufficient for our present purpose, if we have proved, that the taste of all individuals is not upon an equal footing, and that some men in general, however difficult to be particularly pitched upon, will be acknowledged by universal sentiment to have a preference above others.

But, in reality, the difficulty of finding, even in particulars, the standard of taste, is not so great as it is represented. Though in speculation we may readily avow a certain criterion in science, and deny it in sentiment, the matter is found in practice to be much more hard to ascertain in the former case than in the latter. Theories of abstract philosophy, systems of profound theology, have prevailed during one age; in a successive period these have been universally exploded; their absurdity has been detected; other theories and systems have supplied their place, which again gave place to their successors; and nothing has been experienced more liable to the revolutions of chance and fashion than these pretended decisions of science. The case is not the same with the beauties of eloquence and poetry. Just expressions of passion and nature are sure, after a little time, to gain public applause, which they maintain forever. Aristotle, and Plato, and Epicurus, and Descartes, may successively yield to each other; but Terence and Virgil maintain a universal, undisputed empire over the minds of men. The abstract philosophy of Cicero has lost its credit; the vehemence of his oratory is still the object of our admiration. . . .

But notwithstanding all our endeavors to fix a standard of taste, and reconcile the discordant apprehensions of men, there still remain two sources of variation, which are not sufficient indeed to confound all the boundaries of beauty and deformity, but will often serve to produce a difference in the degrees of our approbation or blame. The one is the different humors of particular men; the other, the particular manners and opinions of our age and country. The general principles of taste are uniform in human nature: where men vary in their judgments, some defect or perversion in the faculties may commonly be remarked; proceeding either from prejudice, from want of practice, or want of delicacy; and there is just reason for approving one taste, and condemning another. But where there is such a diversity in the internal frame or external situation as is entirely blameless on both sides, and leaves no room to give one the preference above the other; in that case a certain degree of diversity in judgment is unavoidable, and we seek in vain for a standard, by which we can reconcile the contrary sentiments.

A young man, whose passions are warm, will be more sensibly touched with amorous and tender images, than a man more advanced in years, who takes pleasure in wise, philosophical reflections, concerning the conduct of life, and moderation of the passions. At twenty, Ovid may be the favorite author, Horace at forty, and perhaps Tacitus at fifty. Vainly would we, in such cases, endeavor to enter into the sentiments of others, and divest ourselves of those propensities which are natural to us. We choose our favorite author as we do our friend, from a conformity of humor and disposition. Mirth or passion, sentiment or reflection; whichever of these most predominates in our temper, it gives us a peculiar sympathy with the writer who resembles us.

One person is more pleased with the sublime, another with the tender, a third with raillery. . . . The ear of this man is entirely turned towards conciseness and energy; that man is delighted with a copious, rich, and harmonious expression. Simplicity is affected by one; ornament by another. Comedy, tragedy, satire, odes, have each its partisans, who prefer that particular species of writing to all others. It is plainly an error in a critic, to confine his approbation to one species or style of writing, and condemn all the rest. But it is almost impossible not to feel a predilection for that which suits our particular turn and disposition. Such performances are innocent and unavoidable, and can never reasonably be the object of dispute, because there is no standard by which they can be decided.

For a like reason, we are more pleased, in the course of our reading, with pictures and characters that resemble objects which are found in our own age and country, than with those which describe a different set of customs. It is not without some effort that we reconcile ourselves to the simplicity of ancient manners, and behold princesses carrying water from the spring, and kings and heroes dressing their own victuals. . . .

Where the idea of morality and decency alter from one age to another, and where vicious manners are described, without being marked with the proper characters of blame and disapprobation, this must be allowed to disfigure the poem, and to be a real deformity. I cannot, nor is it proper I should, enter into such sentiments; and however I may excuse the poet, on account of the manners of his age, I can never relish the composition. The want of humanity and of decency, so conspicuous in the characters drawn by several of the ancient poets, even sometimes by Homer and the Greek tragedians, diminishes considerably the merit of their noble performances. . . .

The case is not the same with moral principles as with speculative opinions of any kind. Speculative opinions . . . are in continual flux and revolution. The son embraces a different system from the father. Nay, there scarcely is any man, who can boast of great constancy and uniformity in this particular. Whatever speculative errors may be found in the polite writings of any age or country, they detract but little from the value of those compositions. . . .

Of all speculative errors, those which regard religion are the most excusable in compositions of genius; nor is it ever permitted to judge of the civility or wisdom of any people, or even of single persons, by the grossness or refinement of their theological principles. The same good sense that directs men in the ordinary occurrences of life, is not hearkened to in religious matters, which are supposed to be placed altogether above the cognizance of human reason. On this account, all the absurdities of the pagan system of theology must be overlooked by every critic, who would pretend to form a just notion of ancient poetry; and our posterity, in their turn, must have the same indulgence to their forefathers. No religious principles can ever be imputed as a fault to any poet, while they remain merely principles, and take not such strong possession of his heart as to lay him under the imputation of *bigotry* or *superstition*. Where that happens, they confound the sentiments of morality, and alter the natural boundaries of vice and virtue. They are therefore eternal blemishes, according to the principle above mentioned; nor are the prejudices and false opinions of the age sufficient to justify them.

It is essential to the Roman Catholic religion to inspire a violent hatred of every other worship, and to represent all pagans, Mahometans, and heretics, as the objects of divine wrath and vengeance. Such sentiments, though they are in reality very blamable, are considered as virtues by the zealots of that communion, and are represented in their tragedies and epic poems as a kind of divine heroism. This bigotry has disfigured two very fine tragedies of the French theatre, Polieucte and Athalia; where an intemperate zeal for particular modes of worship is set off with all the pomp imaginable, and forms the predominant character of the heroes. "What is this," says the sublime Joad to Josabet, finding her in discourse with Mathan the priest of Baal, "Does the daughter of David speak to this traitor? Are you not afraid lest the earth should open, and pour forth flames to devour you both? Or lest these holy walls should fall and crush you together? What is his purpose? Why comes that enemy of God hither to poison the air, which we breathe, with his horrid presence?" Such sentiments are received with great applause on the theatre of Paris; but at London the spectators would be full as much pleased to hear Achilles tell Agamemnon, that he was a dog in his forehead, and a deer in his heart; or Jupiter threaten Juno with a sound drubbing, if she will not be quiet.

Religious principles are also a blemish in any polite composition, when they rise up to superstition, and intrude themselves into every sentiment, however remote from any connection with religion. It is no excuse for the poet, that the customs of his country had burdened life with so many religious ceremonies and observances, that no part of it was exempt from that yoke. It must forever be ridiculous in Petrarch to compare his mistress, Laura, to Jesus Christ. Nor is it less ridiculous in that agreeable libertine, Boccace, very seriously to give thanks to God Almighty and the ladies, for their assistance in defending him against his enemies.

Of Refinement in the Arts

Luxury is a word of an uncertain signification, and may be taken in a good as well as in a bad sense. . . . The bounds between the virtue and the vice cannot here be exactly fixed, more than in other moral subjects. To imagine, that the gratifying of any sense, or the indulging of any delicacy in meat, drink, or apparel, is of itself a vice, can never enter into a head, that is not disordered by the frenzies of enthusiasm. . . . Indulgences are only vices, when they are pursued at the expense of some virtue, as liberality or charity; in like manner as they are follies, when for them a man ruins his fortune, and reduces himself to want and beggary. Where they entrench upon no virtue, but leave ample subject whence to provide for friends, family, and every proper object of generosity or compassion, they are entirely innocent, and have in every age been acknowledged such by almost all moralists. To be entirely occupied with the luxury of the table, for instance, without any relish for the pleasures of ambition, study, or conversation, is a mark of stupidity, and is incompatible with any vigor of temper or genius. To confine one's expense entirely to such a gratification, without regard to friends or family, is an indication of a heart destitute of humanity or benevolence. But if a man reserve time sufficient for all laudable pursuits, and money sufficient for all generous purposes, he is free from every shadow of blame or reproach. . . .

. . . Human happiness, according to the most received notions, seems to consist in three ingredients: action, pleasure, and indolence; and though these ingredients ought to be mixed in different proportions, according to the particular disposition of the person; yet no one ingredient can be entirely wanting, without destroying, in some measure, the relish of the whole composition. Indolence or repose, indeed, seems not of itself to contribute much to our enjoyment; but, like sleep, is requisite as an indulgence, to the weakness of human nature, which cannot support an uninterrupted course of business or pleasure. . . .

The more these refined arts advance, the more sociable men become; nor is it possible, that, when enriched with science, and possessed of a fund of conversation, they should be contented to remain in solitude, or live with their fellow-citizens in that distant manner, which is peculiar to ignorant and barbarous nations. They flock into cities; love to receive and communicate knowledge; to show their wit or their breeding; their taste in conversation or living, in clothes or furniture. Curiosity allures the wise; vanity the foolish; and pleasure both. Particular clubs and societies are everywhere formed; both sexes meet in an easy and sociable manner; and the tempers of men, as well as their behavior, refine apace. . . .

... The more men refine upon pleasure, the less will they indulge in excesses of any kind; because nothing is more destructive to true pleasure than such excesses. ...

What has chiefly induced severe moralists to declaim against refinement in the arts, is the example of ancient Rome. ...

But it would be easy to prove, that these writers mistook the cause of the disorders in the Roman state, and ascribed to luxury and the arts, what really proceeded from an ill-modelled government, and the unlimited extent of conquests. Refinement on the pleasures and conveniences of life has no natural tendency to beget venality and corruption. The value which all men put upon any particular pleasure, depends on comparison and experience; nor is a porter less greedy of money, which he spends on bacon and brandy, than a courtier, who purchases champagne and ortolans. Riches are valuable at all times, and to all men; because they always purchase pleasures, such as men are accustomed to and desire; nor can anything restrain or regulate the love of money, but a sense of honor and virtue; which, if it be not nearly equal at all times, will naturally abound most in ages of knowledge and refinement. ...

Luxury, when excessive, is the source of many ills, but is in general preferable to sloth and idleness, which would commonly succeed in its place, and are more hurtful both to private persons and to the public. When sloth reigns, a mean uncultivated way of life prevails amongst individuals, without society, without enjoyment. . . .

Of the Original Contract

All *moral* duties may be divided into two kinds. The *first* are those to which men are impelled by a natural instinct or immediate propensity which operates on them, independent of all ideas of obligation, and of all views either to public or private utility. Of this nature are love of children, gratitude to benefactors, pity to the unfortunate. When we reflect on the advantage which results to society from such humane instincts, we pay them the just tribute of moral approbation and esteem; but the person actuated by them feels their power and influence antecedent to any such reflection.

The *second* kind of moral duties are such as are not supported by any original instinct of nature, but are performed entirely from a sense of obligation, when we consider the necessities of human society, and the impossibility of supporting it, if these duties were neglected. It is thus *justice*, or a regard to the property of others, *fidelity*, or the observance of promises, become obligatory, and acquire an authority over mankind. For as it is evident that every man loves himself better than any other person, he is naturally impelled to extend his acquisitions as much as possible; and nothing can restrain him in this propensity but reflection and experience, by which he learns the pernicious effects of that license, and the total dissolution of society which must ensue from it. His original inclination, therefore, or instinct, is here checked and restrained by a subsequent judgment or observation.

The case is precisely the same with the political or civil duty of *allegiance* as with the natural duties of justice and fidelity. Our primary instincts lead us either to indulge ourselves in unlimited freedom, or to seek dominion over others; and it is reflection only which engages us to sacrifice such strong passions to the interests of peace and public order. A small degree of experience and observation suffices to teach us, that society cannot possibly be maintained without the authority of magistrates, and that this authority must soon fall into contempt where exact obedience is not paid to it. The observation of these general and obvious interests is the source of all allegiance, and of that moral obligation which we attribute to it.

What necessity, therefore, is there to found the duty of *allegiance*, or obedience to magistrates, on that of *fidelity*, or a regard to promises, and to suppose that it is the consent of each individual which subjects him to government, when it appears that both allegiance and fidelity stand precisely on the same foundation, and are both submitted to by mankind, on account of the apparent interests and necessities of human society? We are bound to obey our sovereign, it is said, because we have given a tacit promise to that purpose. But why are we bound to observe our promise? It must here be asserted, that the commerce and intercourse of mankind, which are of such mighty advantage, can have no security where men pay no regard to their engagements. In like manner may it be said that men could not live at all in society, at least in a civilized society, without laws, and magistrates, and judges, to prevent the encroachments of the strong upon the weak, of the violent upon the just and equitable. The obligation to allegiance being of like force and authority with the obligation to fidelity, we gain nothing by resolving the one into the other. The general interests or necessities of society are sufficient to establish both. . . .

We shall only observe, before we conclude, that though an appeal to general opinion may justly, in the speculative sciences of metaphysics, natural philosophy, or astronomy, be deemed unfair and inconclusive, yet in all questions with regard to morals, as well as criticism, there is really no other standard, by which any controversy can ever be decided. And nothing is a clearer proof, that a theory of this kind is erroneous, than to find, that it leads to paradoxes repugnant to the common sentiments of mankind, and to the practice and opinion of all nations and all ages. . . .

Of the Delicacy of Taste and Passion

Philosophers have endeavored to render happiness entirely independent of everything external. This degree of perfection is impossible to be *attained*; but every wise man will endeavor to place his happiness on such objects chiefly as depend upon himself. . . .

Of the Dignity or Meanness of Human Nature

In my opinion, there are two things which have led astray those philosophers that have insisted so much on the selfishness of man. In the *first* place, they found that every act of virtue or friendship was attended with a secret pleasure; whence they concluded, that friendship and virtue could not be disinterested. But the fallacy of this is obvious. The virtuous sentiment or passion produces the pleasure, and does not arise from it. I feel a pleasure in doing good to my friend, because I love him; but do not love him for the sake of that pleasure.

In the *second* place, it has always been found, that the virtuous are far from being indifferent to praise; and therefore they have been represented as a set of vainglorious men, who had nothing in view but the applauses of others. But this also is a fallacy. It is very unjust in the world, when they find any tincture of vanity in a laudable action, to depreciate it upon that account, or ascribe it entirely to that motive. The case is not the same with vanity, as with other passions. Where avarice or revenge enters into any seemingly virtuous action, it is difficult for us to determine how far it enters, and it is natural to suppose it the sole actuating principle. But vanity is so closely allied to virtue, and to love the fame of laudable actions approaches so near the love of laudable actions for their own sake, that these passions are more capable of mixture, than any other kinds of affection; and it is almost impossible to have the latter without some degree of the former. Accordingly we find, that this passion for glory is always warped and varied according to the particular taste or disposition of the mind on which it falls. Nero had the same vanity in driving a chariot, that Trajan had in governing the empire with justice and ability. To love the glory of virtuous deeds is a sure proof of the love of virtue.

The Epicurean

If life be frail, if youth be transitory, we should well employ the present moment, and lose no part of so perishable an existence. Yet a little moment, and *these* shall be no more. We shall be as if we had never been.

Not a memory of us be left upon earth; and even the fabulous shades below will not afford us a habitation. Our fruitless anxieties, our vain projects, our uncertain speculations, shall all be swallowed up and lost. Our present doubts, concerning the original cause of all things, must never, alas! be resolved. This alone we may be certain of, that if any governing mind preside, he must be pleased to see us fulfill the ends of our being, and enjoy that pleasure for which alone we were created. Let this reflection give ease to your anxious thoughts; but render not your joys too serious, by dwelling forever upon it. It is sufficient once to be acquainted with this philosophy, in order to give an unbounded loose to love and jollity, and remove all the scruples of a vain superstition. . . .

The Stoic

In vain do you seek repose from beds of roses: in vain do you hope for enjoyment from the most delicious wines and fruits. Your indolence itself becomes a fatigue; your pleasure itself creates disgust. The mind, unexercised, finds every delight insipid and loathsome; and ere yet the body, full of noxious humors, feels the torment of its multiplied diseases, your nobler part is sensible of the invading poison, and seeks in vain to relieve its anxiety by new pleasures, which still augment the fatal malady.

I need not tell you, that, by this eager pursuit of pleasure, you more and more expose yourself to fortune and accidents, and rivet your affections on external objects, which chance may, in a moment, ravish from you. I shall suppose that your indulgent stars favor you still with the enjoyment of your riches and possessions. I prove to you, that, even in the midst of your luxurious pleasures, you are unhappy; and that, by too much indulgence, you are incapable of enjoying what prosperous fortune still allows you to possess.

But surely the instability of fortune is a consideration not to be overlooked or neglected. Happiness cannot possibly exist where there is no security; and security can have no place where fortune has any dominion. Though that unstable deity should not exert her rage against you, the dread of it would still torment you; would disturb your slumbers, haunt your dreams, and throw a damp on the jollity of your most delicious banquets.

The temple of wisdom is seated on a rock, above the rage of the fighting elements, and inaccessible to all the malice of man. The rolling thunder breaks below; and those more terrible instruments of human fury reach not to so sublime a height. The sage, while he breathes that serene air, looks down with pleasure, mixed with compassion, on the errors of mistaken mortals, who blindly seek for the true path of life, and pursue riches, nobility, honor, or power, for genuine felicity. The greater part he beholds disappointed of their fond wishes: some lament, that having once possessed the object of their desires, it is ravished from them by envious fortune; and all complain, that even their own vows, though granted, cannot give them happiness, or relieve the anxiety of their distracted minds.

But does the sage always preserve himself in this philosophical indifference, and rest contented with lamenting the miseries of mankind, without ever employing himself for their relief? Does he constantly indulge this severe wisdom, which, by pretending to elevate him above human accidents, does in reality harden his heart, and render him careless of the interests of mankind, and of society? No; he knows that in this sullen *Apathy* neither true wisdom nor true happiness can be found. He feels too strongly the charm of the social affections, ever to counteract so sweet, so natural, so virtuous a propensity. . . .

Proceed still in purifying the generous passions, you will still the more admire its shining glories. What charms are there in the harmony of minds, and in a friendship founded on mutual esteem and gratitude! What satisfaction in relieving the distressed, in comforting the afflicted, in raising the fallen, and in stopping the career of cruel fortune, or of more cruel man, in their insults over the good and virtuous! . . .

But these objects are still too limited for the human mind, which, being of celestial origin, swells with the divinest and most enlarged affections, and, carrying its attention beyond kindred and acquaintance, extends its benevolent wishes to the most distant posterity. It views liberty and laws as the source of human happiness, and devotes itself, with the utmost alacrity, to their guardianship and protection. Toils, dangers, death itself, carry their charms, when we brave them for the public good, and ennoble that being which we generously sacrifice for the interests of our country. Happy the man whom indulgent fortune allows to pay to virtue what he owes to nature, and to make a generous gift of what must otherwise be ravished from him by cruel necessity! . . .

The Platonist

How can a rational soul, made for the contemplation of the Supreme Being, and of his works, ever enjoy tranquility or satisfaction, while detained in the ignoble pursuits of sensual pleasure or popular applause? The divinity is a boundless ocean of bliss and glory: human minds are smaller streams, which, arising at first from this ocean, seek still, amid all their wanderings, to return to it, and to lose themselves in that immensity of perfection. When checked in this natural course by vice or folly, they become furious and enraged; and, swelling to a torrent, do then spread horror and devastation on the neighboring plains. . . .

The most perfect happiness surely must arise from the contemplation of the most perfect object. But what more perfect than beauty and virtue? . . .

Part Three

Economics

Brief Introduction: What David Hume Has to Teach Us Today

READING **D**AVID **H**UME (1711–1776) on economics, one has the feeling that he is rebutting today's dominant Keynesian policies, the policies espoused by almost all world governments of our era. But how can this be, since Hume died in 1776 and Keynes in 1946? The explanation is simple: Keynesianism is not really new. It is in large part a revival of the old mercantilist ideas that Hume was vigorously attacking.

Keynes acknowledges at the end of his magnum opus, *The General Theory of Employment, Interest, and Money*, that he is reviving mercantilism. This is a bit unexpected by the reader, because earlier in the same book he states that he is staking out new ground in economics, but perhaps he means that he is staking out new ground by reviving and updating mercantilism. Whatever the explanation, much of Hume seems highly relevant to current debates for and against Keynes, a proponent of government deficit spending to stimulate a weak economy and of government control of the money supply in order to bring down interest rates. On trade issues, Keynes took different positions at different times. He began as a Humean free trader, then became a protectionist, then returned to a generally free trade position after World War II.

Here is a little of what Hume actually said about these matters:

On Deficit Spending

> ... Our modern expedient, which has become very general, is to mortgage the public revenues, and to trust that posterity will pay off the encumbrances contracted by their ancestors: ... [This is] ... a ... ruinous ... practice....

> It is very tempting to a minister to employ such an expedient, as it enables him to make a great figure during his administration, without overburdening the people with taxes, or exciting any immediate clamors against himself. The practice, therefore,

of contracting debt, will almost infallibly be abused in every government. It would scarcely be more imprudent to give a prodigal son a credit in every banker's shop in London, than to empower a statesman to draw bills, in this manner, upon posterity.

What, then, shall we say to the new paradox, that public encumbrances are, of themselves, advantageous, independent of the necessity of contracting them.... [These] ... absurd maxims [are] patronized by great ministers, and by a whole party among us. ...

It must, indeed, be one of these two events: either the nation must destroy public credit, or public credit will destroy the nation. It is impossible that they can both subsist.... ("Of Public Credit")

On Money and Banking

... A government has great reason to preserve with care its people and its manufactures. Its money, it may safely trust to the course of human affairs. ...

We fancy, because an individual would be much richer, were his stock of money doubled, that the same good effect would follow, were the money of every one increased; not considering that this would raise as much the price of every commodity, and reduce every man in time to the same condition as before.... ("Of the Balance of Trade")

It is also evident, that the prices do not so much depend on the absolute quantity of commodities and that of money, which are in a nation, as on that of the commodities, which come or may come to market, and of the money which circulates. . . .

Though the high price of commodities be a necessary consequence of the increase of gold and silver, yet it follows not immediately upon that increase; but some time is required before the money circulates through the whole state, and makes its effect be felt on all ranks of people. At first, no alteration is perceived; by degrees the price rises, first of one commodity, then of another till the whole at last reaches a just proportion with the new quantity of specie which is in the kingdom.

Institutions of banks, funds, and paper credit, with which we in the Kingdom are so much infatuated, … render paper equivalent to money, [and] circulate it through the whole state.… What can be more short-sighted than our reasoning on this head.…

It must be allowed that no bank would be more advantageous, than such alone as … never augmented the circulating coin." ("Of Money") [Hume pointed with admiration to the Bank of Amsterdam that was run at the time on 100% reserve lines.]

On Trade

Nothing is more usual, among states which have made some advances in commerce, than to look on the progress of their neighbors with a suspicious eye, to consider all trading states as their rivals, and to suppose that it is impossible for any of them to flourish, but at their expense. In opposition to this narrow and malignant opinion, I will venture to assert, that the increase of riches and commerce in any one nation, instead of hurting, commonly promotes the riches and commerce of all its neighbors; and that a state can scarcely carry its trade and industry very far, where all the surrounding states are buried in

ignorance, sloth, and barbarism.... ("Of
the Balance of Trade")

On the Theory of Value

When Hume received a copy of Adam Smith's *Wealth
of Nations* during his final illness, he immediately saw
the error of Smith's labor theory of value:

> If you were at my fireside, I should dispute
> some of your principles. I cannot think...
> but that... price is determined altogether
> by the quantity and the demand.*

On the Need for Better Economic Thinking

> Mankind are, in all ages, caught by the same
> baits: the same tricks played over and over
> again, still trepan them. ("Of Public Credit")

> ... It must be owned, that nothing can be of
> more use than to improve, by practice, the
> method of reasoning on these subjects, which
> of all others are the most important, though
> they are commonly treated in the loosest
> and most careless manner. ("Of Interest")

---

* E. Rotwein ed., Letter to Adam Smith, April 1, 1776, Hume's Correspondence, *Writings on Economics*, (Madison, WI: The University of
Wisconsin Press, 1955), 217.

Hume was one of the great classical liberals of European history, which in today's language would make him in economics a proponent of unfettered markets and in politics a libertarian.

—Hunter Lewis

Introduction

ALTHOUGH DAVID HUME is best known as a philosopher, he was also a penetrating and important economist. Some of his most important insights may be summarized as follows:

1. It is not money that makes a society rich.

Since wealth is measured in money, it is easy to confuse the two. But it is the ability to produce that makes us rich. If we add to the money supply without increasing the ability to produce, the result will just be higher prices. As Hume explains:

> We fancy, because an individual would be much richer, were his stock of money doubled, that the same good effect would follow, were the money of every one increased; not considering that this would

raise as much the price of every commodity, and reduce every man in time to the same condition as before.... ("Of the Balance of Trade")

The prices of everything depend on the proportion between commodities and money, and . . . any considerable alteration on either has the same effect, either of heightening or lowering the price. Increase the commodities, they become cheaper; increase the money, they rise in their value.

It is also evident, that the prices do not so much depend on the absolute quantity of commodities and that of money, which are in a nation, as on that of the commodities, which come or may come to market, and of the money which circulates. If the coin be locked up in chests, it is the same thing with regard to prices, as if it were annihilated; if the commodities be hoarded in magazines and granaries, a like effect follows. As the money and commodities, in these cases, never meet, they cannot affect each other.

The necessary effect is, that, provided the money increase not in the nation, everything must become much cheaper in times

> of industry and refinement, than in rude,
> uncultivated ages.... ("Of Money")

Hume makes it clear that falling prices are a dividend of industry and should not be feared. Nor is it necessary for authorities to keep creating new money as an economy grows:

> Here then we may learn the fallacy of the
> remark, often to be met with in historians,
> and even in common conversation, that
> any particular state is weak, though fertile,
> populous, and well cultivated, merely because it wants money. It appears, that the
> want of money can never injure any state
> within itself: For men and commodities
> are the real strength of any community.
> ("Of Money")

Hume did, however, add a caveat to the idea that money is "neutral," that what matters is not the amount of money in circulation but rather a society's ability to produce. He noted that new money does not tend to fall into everyone's hands at once or evenly. New money often falls into the hands of a few people who have first use of it—before it has flowed into the economy and raised prices. Anyone with access to new money before it has altered economic calculations clearly has an advantage, because these fortunate people can use the new money to buy at pre-inflation prices. Because the process of injecting new money into an economy is not "neutral," it is unfair to most people:

> Though the high price of commodities be a necessary consequence of the increase of gold and silver, yet it follows not immediately upon that increase; but some time is required before the money circulates through the whole state, and makes its effect be felt on all ranks of people. At first, no alteration is perceived; by degrees the price rises, first of one commodity, then of another till the whole at last reaches a just proportion with the new quantity of specie which is in the kingdom. In my opinion, it is only in this interval or intermediate situation, between the acquisition of money and rise of prices, that the increasing quantity of gold and silver is favorable to industry. When any quantity of money is imported into a nation, it is not at first dispersed into many hands, but is confined to the coffers of a few persons, who immediately seek to employ it to advantage. ("Of Money")

2. Interest rates are affected by the quantity of money in an economy, but ultimately reflect other factors as well.

Prices have risen near four times since the discovery of the Indies; and it is probable gold and silver have multiplied much more: but interest has not fallen much above half. The rate of interest, therefore, is not derived [solely] . . . from the quantity of the precious metals. . . .

High interest arises from *three* circumstances: a great demand for borrowing, little riches to supply that demand, and great profits arising from commerce: and the circumstances are a clear proof of the small advance of commerce and industry, not of the scarcity of gold and silver. Low interest, on the other hand, proceeds from the three opposite circumstances: a small demand for borrowing; great riches to supply that demand; and small profits arising from commerce. . . .

. . . Suppose that, by miracle, every man in Great Britain should have five pounds slipped into his pocket in one night; this would much more than double the whole money that is at present in the kingdom; yet there would not next day, nor for some time, be any more lenders, nor any variation in the interest. And were there nothing but landlords and peasants in the state, this money, however abundant, could never gather into sums, and would only serve to increase the prices of everything, without any further consequence. . . .

A . . . reason of . . . [the] popular mistake with regard to the cause of low interest, seems to be the instance of some nations, where, after a sudden acquisition of money, or of the precious metals by means of foreign conquest, the interest has fallen not only among them, but in all the neighboring states, as soon as that money was dispersed, and had insinuated itself into every corner. Thus, interest in Spain fell near a half immediately after the discovery of the West Indies, as we are informed by Garcilasso de la Vega; and it has been ever since gradually sinking in every kingdom of Europe. . . .

In the conquering country, it is natural to imagine that this new acquisition of money will fall into a few hands, and be gathered into large sums, which seek a secure revenue, either by the purchase of land or by interest; and consequently the same effect follows, for a little time, as if there had been a great accession of industry and commerce. The increase of lenders above the borrowers sinks the interest, and so much the faster if those who have acquired those large sums find no industry or commerce in the state, and no method of employing their money but by lending it at interest.

But after this new mass of gold and silver has been digested, and has circulated through the whole state, affairs will soon return to their former situation, while the landlords and new money-holders, living idly, squander above their income; and the former daily contract debt, and the latter encroach on their stock till its final extinction. The whole money may still be in the state, and make itself felt by the increase of prices; but not being now collected into any large masses or stocks, the disproportion between the borrowers and lenders is the same as formerly, and consequently the high interest returns. . . . ("Of Interest")

Hume goes on to explain that interest can only be lowered over the long run, not by financial manipulations, but by increasing production. As production increases, producer profits will also fall:

... It must be owned, that nothing can be of more use than to improve, by practice, the method of reasoning on these subjects, which of all others are the most important, though they are commonly treated in the loosest and most careless manner.

An increase of commerce, by a necessary consequence, raises a great number of lenders, and by that means produces lowness of interest. We must now consider how far this increase of commerce diminishes the profits arising from that profession, and gives rise to the *third* circumstance requisite to produce lowness of interest. ...

When commerce has become extensive, and employs large stocks, there must arise rivalries among the merchants, which diminish the profits of trade, at the same time that they increase the trade itself. The low profits of merchandise induce the merchants to accept more willingly of a low interest when they leave off business, and begin to indulge themselves in ease and indolence. It is needless, therefore, to inquire, which of these circumstances, to wit, *low interest* or *low profits*, is the cause, and which the effect? They both arise from an extensive commerce, and mutually forward each other. . . .

No man will accept of low profits where he can have high interest; and no man will accept of low interest where he can have high profits. An extensive commerce, by producing large stocks, diminishes both interest and profits, and is always assisted, in its diminution of the one, by the proportional sinking of the other. I may add, that, as low profits arise from the increase of commerce and industry, they serve in their turn to its further increase, by rendering the commodities cheaper, encouraging the consumption, and heightening the industry. And thus, if we consider the whole connection of causes and effects, interest is the barometer of the state, and its lowness is a sign, almost infallible, of the flourishing condition of a people. . . . ("Of Interest")

Hume adds a comment which sheds much light on why economic fallacies are revived over and over through the ages, even after they have been thoroughly refuted:

It must be owned, that nothing can be of more use than to improve, by practice, the method of reasoning on these [economic] subjects, which of all others are the most important, though they are commonly treated in the loosest and most careless manner. ("Of Interest")

3. **Paper money, whether issued by governments or banks, is injurious to an economy, because it leads to price inflation. The practice whereby banks are allowed to create the equivalent of paper money by lending money they do not possess (fractional reserve banking) should be abolished.**

Institutions of banks, funds, and paper credit, with which we in the Kingdom are so much infatuated, ... render paper equivalent to money, circulate it through the whole state, make it supply the place of gold and silver, raise proportionately the price of labor and commodities, and by that means ... banish a great part of those precious metals. . . . What can be more short-sighted than our reasoning on this head ... [since the production of this faux money just] raise[s] the price of every commodity.

It must be allowed that no bank would be more advantageous, than such alone as . . . never augmented the circulating coin. ("Of Money")

Hume even pointed to the Bank of Amsterdam that was run on these 100% reserve lines. It kept custody of funds and lent money out as agent for the owner, but never lent money it did not possess, and therefore did not create new money as banks continue to do to this day.

4. Commodities are worth what someone will pay for them, not what they cost to produce.

Hume's friend Adam Smith claimed the opposite in his *Wealth of Nations*. This error was in turn reproduced in Karl Marx's labor theory of value, where it had an immense impact on Communist doctrine and therefore on world history. Hume caught the error when, close to dying, he received an early copy of *Wealth of Nations*. It took other economists another century to realize that Hume was right and Smith wrong. By then Marx's Communism was already a well-established ideology.

Smith in earlier years had been something of a protégé of Hume's, and held views closer to his mentor's. Smith's embrace of fractional reserve banking in *Wealth of Nations*, contrary to Hume's teaching, also had an immense impact on subsequent world history, because the resulting fragility of the banking system greatly contributed to cycles of boom and bust that plagued the global market system.

5. Foreign trade does not mean "Beggar Thy Neighbor."

Hume forcefully argued that international trade is not a ruthless competition, a zero sum game in which the gains of one nation can only come at the expense of another. It should least of all be seen as an extension of war by other means, and should not even be considered "an affair of state." ("Of Civil Liberty") On the contrary, trade is advantageous for both parties; both parties should equally be winners:

> Nothing is more usual, among states which have made some advances in commerce, than to look on the progress of their neighbors with a suspicious eye, to consider all trading states as their rivals, and to suppose that it is impossible for any of them to flourish, but at their expense. In opposition to this narrow and malignant opinion, I will venture to assert, that the increase of riches and commerce in any one nation, instead of hurting, commonly promotes the riches and commerce of all its neighbors; and that a state can scarcely carry its trade and industry very far, where all the surrounding states are buried in ignorance, sloth, and barbarism. . . .

I shall therefore venture to acknowledge, that, not only as a man, but as a British subject, I pray for the flourishing commerce of Germany, Spain, Italy, and even France itself. I am at least certain, that Great Britain, and all those nations, would flourish more, did their sovereigns and ministers adopt such enlarged and benevolent sentiments towards each other. . . . ("Of the Balance of Trade")

Hume also exploded the idea that the purpose of trade was to attract money from trade rivals which could then be hoarded:

These errors, one may say, are gross and palpable; but there still prevails, even in nations well acquainted with commerce, a strong jealousy with regard to the balance of trade, and a fear that all their gold and silver may be leaving them. This seems to me, almost in every case, a groundless apprehension; and I should as soon dread, that all our springs and rivers should be exhausted, as that money should abandon a kingdom where there are people and industry. . . .

Suppose four fifths of all the money in Great Britain to be annihilated in one night, and the nation reduced to the same condition, with regard to specie, as in the reigns of the Harrys and Edwards, what would be the consequence? Must not the price of all labor and commodities sink in proportion, and everything be sold as cheap as they were in those ages? What nation could then dispute with us in any foreign market, or pretend to navigate or to sell manufactures at the same price, which to us would afford sufficient profit? In how little time, therefore, must this bring back the money which we had lost, and raise us to the level of all the neighboring nations? Where, after we have arrived, we immediately lose the advantage of the cheapness of labor and commodities, and the further flowing in of money is stopped by our fullness and repletion.

Again, suppose that all the money of Great Britain were multiplied fivefold in a night, must not the contrary effect follow? Must not all labor and commodities rise to such an exorbitant height, that no neighboring nations could afford to buy from us; while their commodities, on the other hand, became comparatively so cheap, that, in spite of all the laws which could be formed, they would be run in upon us, and our money flow

> out; till we fall to a level with foreigners, and lose that great superiority of riches, which had laid us under such disadvantages? ...
>
> In short, a government has great reason to preserve with care its people and its manufactures. Its money, it may safely trust to the course of human affairs, without fear or jealousy.... ("Of the Balance of Trade")

This important observation was not entirely original to Hume. Isaac Gervais discovered the truth of it a few years earlier, but Hume's explanation brought it home to a wider British public. Hume also answered the objection that Britain depended on import taxes for government revenue:

> ... As it is necessary that imposts should be levied for the support of government, it may be thought more convenient to lay them on foreign commodities, which can easily be intercepted at the port, and subjected to the impost. We ought, however, always to remember the maxim of Dr. Swift, that, in the arithmetic of the customs, two and two make not four, but often make only one. It can scarcely be doubted, but if the duties on wine were lowered to a third, they would yield much more to the government than at present.... ("Of the Balance of Trade")

6. The pursuit of wealth is not an evil, but generally good for a society, especially when compared to the alternatives.

This point is not part of economics per se, but Hume's sociological argument is worth noting:

> There is no craving or demand of the human mind more constant and insatiable than that for exercise and employment; and this desire seems the foundation of most of our passions and pursuits. Deprive a man of all business and serious occupation, he runs restless from one amusement to another; and the weight and oppression which he feels from idleness is so great, that he forgets the ruin which must follow him from his immoderate expenses. Give him a more harmless way of employing his mind or body, he is satisfied, and feels no longer that insatiable thirst after pleasure. But if the employment you give him be lucrative, especially if the profit be attached to every particular exertion of industry, he has gain so often in his eye, that he acquires, by degrees, a passion for it, and knows no such pleasure as that of seeing the daily increase of his fortune. And this is the reason why trade increases frugality, and why,

among merchants, there is the same over-
plus of misers above prodigals, as among
the possessors of land there is the contrary.
("Of Interest")

Hume also expressed admiration for merchants, whose occupation was looked down upon at that time in Britain:

Merchants [are] ... one of the most useful races of men, who serve as agents between those parts of the state that are wholly un-acquainted, and are ignorant of each other's necessities.... ("Of Interest")

7. Government borrowing that is never repaid is an evil.

Government borrowing and borrowing anew to repay old debts, which are thus never really paid off, was a new idea in Hume's day. He thought it would end badly:

... Our modern expedient, which has be-come very general, is to mortgage the public revenues, and to trust that posterity will pay off the encumbrances contracted by their an-cestors: and they, having before their eyes so good an example of their wise fathers, have the same prudent reliance on *their* poster-ity; who, at last, from necessity more than choice, are obliged to place the same confidence in a new posterity.... [This is] ... a practice which appears ruinous beyond all controversy. ...

It is very tempting to a minister to employ such an expedient, as enables him to make a great figure during his administration, without overburdening the people with taxes, or exciting any immediate clamors against himself. The practice, therefore, of contracting debt, will almost infallibly be abused in every government. It would scarcely be more imprudent to give a prodigal son a credit in every banker's shop in London, than to empower a statesman to draw bills, in this manner, upon posterity.

What, then, shall we say to the new paradox, that public encumbrances are, of themselves, advantageous, independent of the necessity of contracting them.... Reasonings such as these might naturally have passed for trials of wit among [ancient] ... rhetoricians, had we not seen such absurd maxims patronized by great ministers, and by a whole party among us. ...

[We are told that] ... public securities are with us become a kind of money, and pass as readily at the current price as gold or silver.... In short our national debts furnish merchants with a species of money that is continually multiplying in their hands, and produces sure gain, besides the profits of their commerce....

We have indeed been told, that the public is no weaker on account of its debts, since they are mostly due among ourselves, and bring as much property to one as they take from another. It is like transferring money from the right hand to the left, which leaves the person neither richer nor poorer than before. Such loose reasoning and specious comparisons will always pass where we judge not upon principles. I ask, "Is it possible, in the nature of things, to overburden a nation with taxes.... But if all our present taxes be mortgaged, must we not invent new ones? And may not this matter be carried to a length that is ruinous and destructive?"...

It must, indeed, be one of these two events; either the nation must destroy public credit, or public credit will destroy the nation. It is impossible that they can both subsist....

It is not altogether improbable, that when the nation becomes heartily sick of their debts, and is cruelly oppressed by them, some daring projector may arise with visionary schemes for their discharge. And as public credit will begin, by that time, to be a little frail, the least touch will destroy it. . . .

Mankind are, in all ages, caught by the same baits: the same tricks played over and over again, still trepan them.

The heights of popularity and patriotism are still the beaten road to power and tyranny; flattery, to treachery; standing armies to arbitrary government; and the glory of God to the temporal interest of the clergy. ("Of Public Credit")

The source of degeneracy which may be remarked in free governments, consists in the practice of contracting debt, and mortgaging the public revenues, by which taxes may, in time, become altogether intolerable. . . . The practice is of modern date. ("Of Civil Liberty")

8. Slavery is an evil, whether regarded morally or from the point of view of economics.

Hume was among the crusaders against the slavery of his time:

> The remains which are found of domestic slavery, in the American colonies, and among some European nations, would never surely create a desire of rendering it more universal. The little humanity commonly observed in persons accustomed, from their infancy, to exercise so great authority over their fellow-creatures, and to trample upon human nature, were sufficient alone to disgust us with that unbounded dominion....
>
> ... Slavery is in general disadvantageous both to the happiness and populousness of mankind, and ... its place is much better supplied by the practice of hired servants. ...
> ("Of the Populousness of Ancient Nations")

9. Humanity needs government for order but government itself must be restrained by laws.

Political Philosophy

Hume is not now much regarded as a political philosopher, although in his own day was best known as the author of a multi-volume history of Britain, which included many important political observations. There are also many political comments from his books and essays worth noting:

> Reserve or disguise . . . are always employed by those who enter upon any new project . . . in . . . government, or endeavor to innovate. . . . ("Of the Protestant Succession")

> We are . . . to look upon all the vast apparatus of our government, as having ultimately no other object or purpose but the distribution of justice. . . .

> All men are sensible of the necessity of justice to maintain peace and order; and all men are sensible of the necessity of peace and order for the maintenance of society. . . . ("Of the Origin of Government")

> It is a question with several, whether there be any essential difference between one form of government and another and, whether every form may not become good or bad, according as it is well or ill administered? . . .

> But here it may be proper to make a distinction. All absolute governments must very much depend on the administration; and this is one of the great inconveniences attending that form of government.

Legislators, therefore, ought not to trust the future government of a state entirely to chance, but ought to provide a system of laws to regulate the administration of public affairs. . . .

. . . Good laws may beget order and moderation in the government, where the manners and customs have instilled little humanity or justice into the tempers of men. . . . ("That Politics May be Reduced to a Science")

. . . It is impossible for the arts and sciences to arise, at first, among any people, unless that people enjoy the blessing of a free government. ("Of the Rise and Progress of the Arts and Sciences")

—HUNTER LEWIS

I

Of Money

I**T IS INDEED** evident, that money is nothing but the representation of labor and commodities, and serves only as a method of rating or estimating them. Where coin is in greater plenty; as a greater quantity of it is required to represent the same quantity of goods; it can have no effect, either good or bad, taking a nation within itself.

To account, then, for this phenomenon, we must consider, that though the high price of commodities be a necessary consequence of the increase of gold and silver, yet it follows not immediately upon that increase; but some time is required before the money circulates through the whole state, and makes its effect be felt on all ranks of people. At first, no alteration is perceived; by degrees the price rises, first of one commodity, then of another till the whole at last reaches a just proportion with the new quantity of specie which is in the kingdom. In my opinion, it is only in this interval or intermediate situation, between the acquisition of money and rise of prices, that the increasing quantity of gold and silver is favorable to industry. When any quantity of money is imported into a nation, it is not at first dispersed into many hands, but is confined to the coffers of a few persons, who immediately seek to employ it to advantage.

It is easy to trace the money in its progress through the whole commonwealth; where we shall find, that it must first quicken the diligence of every individual, before it increases the price of labor.

From the whole of this reasoning we may conclude, that it is of no manner of consequence, with regard to the domestic happiness of a state, whether money be in a greater or less quantity. The good policy of the magistrate consists only in keeping it, if possible, still increasing; because . . . the alterations in the quantity of money, either on one side or the other, are not immediately attended with proportional alterations in the price of commodities. There is always an interval before matters be adjusted to their new situation; and this interval is as pernicious to industry, when gold and silver are diminishing, as it is advantageous when these metals are increasing. The workman has not the same employment from the manufacturer and merchant; though he pays the same price for everything in the market. The farmer cannot dispose of his corn and cattle; though he must pay the same rent to his landlord. The poverty, and beggary, and sloth, which must ensue, are easily foreseen. . . .

It seems a maxim almost self-evident, that the prices of everything depend on the proportion between commodities and money, and that any considerable alteration on either has the same effect, either of heightening or lowering the price. Increase the commodities, they become cheaper; increase the money, they rise in their value.

It is also evident, that the prices do not so much depend on the absolute quantity of commodities and that of money, which are in a nation, as on that of the commodities, which come or may come to market, and of the money which circulates. If the coin be locked up in chests, it is the same thing with regard to prices, as if it were annihilated; if the commodities be hoarded in magazines and granaries, a like effect follows. As the money and commodities, in these cases, never meet, they cannot affect each other.

The necessary effect is, that, provided the money increase not in the nation, everything must become much cheaper in times of industry and refinement, than in rude, uncultivated ages. It is the proportion between the circulating money, and the commodities in the market, which determines the prices.

Here then we may learn the fallacy of the remark, often to be met with in historians, and even in common conversation, that any particular state is weak, though fertile, populous, and well cultivated, merely because it wants money. It appears, that the want of money can never injure any state within itself: For men and commodities are the real strength of any community. ("Of Money")

II

Of Interest

IF THE MULTIPLYING of gold and silver fifteen times makes no difference, much less can the doubling or tripling them. All augmentation has no other effect than to heighten the price of labor and commodities; and even this variation is little more than that of a name. In the progress towards these changes, the augmentation may have some influence, by exciting industry; but after the prices are settled, suitably to the new abundance of gold and silver, it has no manner of influence.

An effect always holds proportion with its cause. Prices have risen near four times since the discovery of the Indies; and it is probable gold and silver have multiplied much more: but interest has not fallen much above half. The rate of interest, therefore, is not derived from the quantity of the precious metals.

Money having chiefly a fictitious value, the greater or less plenty of it is of no consequence, if we consider a nation within itself; and the quantity of specie, when once fixed, though ever so large, has no other effect than to oblige everyone to tell out a greater number of those shining bits of metal for clothes, furniture, or equipage, without increasing any one convenience of life. If a man borrows money to build a house, he then carries home a greater load; because the stone, timber, lead, glass, etc. with the labor of the masons and carpenters, are represented by a greater quantity of gold and silver.

But as these metals are considered chiefly as representations, there can no alteration arise from their bulk or quantity, their weight or color, either upon their real value or their interest. The same interest, in all cases, bears the same proportion to the sum. And if you lent me so much labor and so many commodities, by receiving five *per cent* you always receive proportional labor and commodities, however represented, whether by yellow or white coin, whether by a pound or an ounce. It is in vain, therefore, to look for the cause of the fall or rise of interest in the greater or less quantity of gold and silver, which is fixed in any nation.

High interest arises from *three* circumstances: a great demand for borrowing, little riches to supply that demand, and great profits arising from commerce: and the circumstances are a clear proof of the small advance of commerce and industry, not of the scarcity of gold and silver. Low interest, on the other hand, proceeds from the three opposite circumstances: a small demand for borrowing; great riches to supply that demand; and small profits arising from commerce: and these circumstances are all connected together, and proceed from the increase of industry and commerce, not of gold and silver. We shall endeavor to prove these points; and shall begin with the causes and the effects of a great or small demand for borrowing. . . .

For, suppose that, by miracle, every man in Great Britain should have five pounds slipped into his pocket in one night; this would much more than double the whole money that is at present in the kingdom; yet there would not next day, nor for some time, be any more lenders, nor any variation in the interest. And were there nothing but landlords and peasants in the state, this money, however abundant, could never gather into sums, and would only serve to increase the prices of everything, without any further consequence. . . .

A . . . reason of [the] . . . popular mistake with regard to the cause of low interest, seems to be the instance of some nations, where, after a sudden acquisition of money, or of the precious metals by means of foreign conquest, the interest has fallen not only among them, but in all the neighboring states,

as soon as that money was dispersed, and had insinuated itself into every corner. Thus, interest in Spain
fell near a half immediately after the discovery of the
West Indies, as we are informed by Garcilasso de la
Vega; and it has been ever since gradually sinking in
every kingdom of Europe. . . .

In the conquering country, it is natural to imagine
that this new acquisition of money will fall into a few
hands, and be gathered into large sums, which seek a
secure revenue, either by the purchase of land or by
interest; and consequently the same effect follows,
for a little time, as if there had been a great accession
of industry and commerce. The increase of lenders
above the borrowers sinks the interest, and so much
the faster if those who have acquired those large sums
find no industry or commerce in the state, and no
method of employing their money but by lending it
at interest.

But after this new mass of gold and silver has been
digested, and has circulated through the whole state,
affairs will soon return to their former situation, while
the landlords and new money-holders, living idly,
squander above their income; and the former daily
contract debt, and the latter encroach on their stock
till its final extinction. The whole money may still be in
the state, and make itself felt by the increase of prices;
but not being now collected into any large masses or
stocks, the disproportion between the borrowers and

lenders is the same as formerly, and consequently the high interest returns. . . .

. . . It must be owned, that nothing can be of more use than to improve, by practice, the method of reasoning on these subjects, which of all others are the most important, though they are commonly treated in the loosest and most careless manner.

III

Of Interest, Continued: How Commerce Increases Savings, Lowers Profits, and Lowers Interest, without Ever Requiring the Creation of Additional Money

I N THE INFANCY of society, ... contracts between the artisans and the peasants, and between one species of artisans and another, are commonly entered into immediately by the persons themselves, who, being neighbors, are easily acquainted with each other's necessities, and can lend their mutual assistance to supply them. But when men's industry increases, and their views enlarge, it is found, that the most remote parts of the state can assist each other as well as the more contiguous; and that this inter-course of good offices may be carried on to the great-est extent and intricacy. Hence the origin of *merchants*, one of the most useful races of men, who serve as agents between those parts of the state that are wholly unacquainted, and are ignorant of each other's necessities....

As the people increase in numbers and industry, the difficulty of their intercourse increases: the business of the agency or merchandise becomes more intricate; and divides, subdivides, compounds, and mixes to a greater variety. In all these transactions, it is necessary and reasonable, that a considerable part of the commodities and labor should belong to the merchant, to whom, in a great measure, they are owing. And these commodities he will sometimes preserve in kind, or more commonly convert into money, which is their common representation. If gold and silver have increased in the state, together with the industry, it will require a great quantity of these metals to represent a great quantity of commodities and labor. If industry alone has increased, the prices of everything must sink, and a small quantity of specie will serve as a representation.

There is no craving or demand of the human mind more constant and insatiable than that for exercise and employment; and this desire seems the foundation of most of our passions and pursuits. Deprive a man of all business and serious occupation, he runs restless from one amusement to another; and the weight and oppression which he feels from idleness is so great, that he forgets the ruin which must follow him from his immoderate expenses. Give him a more harmless way of employing his mind or body, he is satisfied, and feels no longer that insatiable thirst after pleasure. But if the employment you give him be lucrative, especially if the profit be attached to every particular exertion of industry, he has gain so often in his eye, that he acquires, by degrees, a passion for it, and knows no such pleasure as that of seeing the daily increase of his fortune. And this is the reason why trade increases frugality, and why, among merchants, there is the same over-plus of misers above prodigals, as among the possessors of land there is the contrary.

Commerce increases industry, by conveying it readily from one member of the state to another, and allowing none of it to perish or become useless. It increases frugality, by giving occupation to men, and employing them in the arts of gain, which soon engage their affection, and remove all relish for pleasure and expense. It is an infallible consequence of all industrious professions to beget frugality, and make the love of gain prevail over the love of pleasure. . . . Lawyers and physicians beget no industry; and it is even at the expense of others they acquire their riches; so that they are sure to diminish the possessions of some of their fellow-citizens, as fast as they increase their own. Merchants, on the contrary, beget industry, by serving as canals to convey it through every corner of the state: and, at the same time, by their frugality, they acquire great power over that industry, and collect a large property in the labor and commodities, which they are the chief instruments in producing. . . .

Thus an increase of commerce, by a necessary consequence, raises a great number of lenders, and by that means produces lowness of interest. We must now consider how far this increase of commerce diminishes the profits arising from that profession, and gives rise to the *third* circumstance requisite to produce lowness of interest. . . .

. . . On the other hand, when commerce has become extensive, and employs large stocks, there must arise rivalries among the merchants, which diminish the profits of trade, at the same time that they increase the trade itself. The low profits of merchandise induce the merchants to accept more willingly of a low interest when they leave off business, and begin to indulge themselves in ease and indolence. It is needless, therefore, to inquire, which of these circumstances, to wit, *low interest* or *low profits*, is the cause, and which the effect? They both arise from an extensive commerce, and mutually forward each other.

No man will accept of low profits where he can have high interest; and no man will accept of low interest where he can have high profits. An extensive commerce, by producing large stocks, diminishes both interest and profits, and is always assisted, in its diminution of the one, by the proportional sinking of the other. I may add, that, as low profits arise from the increase of commerce and industry, they serve in their turn to its further increase, by rendering the commodities cheaper, encouraging the consumption, and heightening the industry. And thus, if we consider the whole connection of causes and effects, interest is the barometer of the state, and its lowness is a sign, almost infallible, of the flourishing condition of a people. . . .

. . . For suppose a nation removed into the Pacific Ocean, without any foreign commerce, or any knowledge of navigation: suppose that this nation possesses always the same stock of coin, but is continually increasing in its numbers and industry: it is evident that the price of every commodity must gradually diminish in that kingdom; since it is the proportion between money and any species of goods which fixes their mutual value; and, upon the present supposition, the conveniences of life become every day more abundant, without any alteration in the current specie. A less quantity of money, therefore, among this people, will make a rich man, during the times of industry, than would suffice to that purpose in ignorant and slothful ages. Less money will build a house, portion a daughter, buy an estate, support a manufactory, or maintain a family and equipage.

IV

Of the Jealousy of Trade

HAVING ENDEAVORED TO remove one species of ill-founded jealousy, which is so prevalent among commercial nations, it may not be amiss to mention another, which seems equally groundless. Nothing is more usual, among states which have made some advances in commerce, than to look on the progress of their neighbors with a suspicious eye, to consider all trading states as their rivals, and to suppose that it is impossible for any of them to flourish, but at their expense. In opposition to this narrow and malignant opinion, I will venture to assert, that the increase of riches and commerce in any one nation, instead of hurting, commonly promotes the riches and commerce of all its neighbors; and that a state can scarcely carry its trade and industry very far, where all the surrounding states are buried in ignorance, sloth, and barbarism. . . .

I shall therefore venture to acknowledge, that, not only as a man, but as a British subject, I pray for the flourishing commerce of Germany, Spain, Italy, and even France itself. I am at least certain, that Great Britain, and all those nations, would flourish more, did their sovereigns and ministers adopt such enlarged and benevolent sentiments towards each other. . . . ("Of the Jealousy of Trade")

V

Of the Balance of Trade

IT IS VERY usual, in nations ignorant of the nature of commerce, to prohibit the exportation of commodities, and to preserve among themselves whatever they think valuable and useful. They do not consider, that in this prohibition they act directly contrary to their intention; and that the more is exported of any commodity, the more will be raised at home, of which they themselves will always have the first offer. . . .

And to this day, in France, the exportation of corn [wheat] is almost always prohibited, in order, as they say, to prevent famines; though it is evident that nothing contributes more to the frequent famines which so much distress that fertile country.

The same jealous fear, with regard to money, has also prevailed among several nations; and it required both reason and experience to convince any people, that these prohibitions serve to no other purpose than to raise the exchange against them, and produce a still greater exportation.

These errors, one may say, are gross and palpable; but there still prevails, even in nations well acquainted with commerce, a strong jealousy with regard to the balance of trade, and a fear that all their gold and silver may be leaving them. This seems to me, almost in every case, a groundless apprehension; and I should as soon dread, that all our springs and rivers should be exhausted, as that money should abandon a kingdom where there are people and industry. Let us carefully preserve these latter advantages, and we need never be apprehensive of losing the former. . . .

Suppose four fifths of all the money in Great Britain to be annihilated in one night, and the nation reduced to the same condition, with regard to specie, as in the reigns of the Harrys and Edwards, what would be the consequence? Must not the price of all labor and commodities sink in proportion, and everything be sold as cheap as they were in those ages? What nation could then dispute with us in any foreign market, or pretend to navigate or to sell manufactures at the same price, which to us would afford sufficient profit? In how little time, therefore, must this bring back the money which we had lost, and raise us to the level of all the neighboring nations? Where, after we have arrived, we immediately lose the advantage of the cheapness of labor and commodities, and the further flowing in of money is stopped by our fullness and repletion.

Again, suppose that all the money of Great Britain were multiplied fivefold in a night, must not the contrary effect follow? Must not all labor and commodities rise to such an exorbitant height, that no neighboring nations could afford to buy from us; while their commodities, on the other hand, became comparatively so cheap, that, in spite of all the laws which could be formed, they would be run in upon us, and our money flow out; till we fall to a level with foreigners, and lose that great superiority of riches, which had laid us under such disadvantages? . . .

Can one imagine that it had ever been possible, by any laws, or even by any art or industry, to have kept all the money in Spain, which the galleons have brought from the Indies? Or that all commodities could be sold in France for a tenth of the price which they would yield on the other side of the Pyrenees, without finding their way thither, and draining from that immense treasure? What other reason, indeed, is there, why all nations at present gain in their trade with Spain and Portugal, but because it is impossible to heap up money, more than any fluid, beyond its proper level? The sovereigns of these countries have shown, that they wanted not inclination to keep their gold and silver to themselves, had it been in any degree practicable. . . .

How is the balance kept in the provinces of every kingdom among themselves, but by the force of this principle, which makes it impossible for money to lose its level, and either to rise or sink beyond the proportion of the labor and commodities which are in each province? . . .

. . . And any man who travels over Europe at this day, may see, by the prices of commodities, that money, in spite of the absurd jealousy of princes and states, has brought itself nearly to a level; and that the difference between one kingdom and another is not greater in this respect, than it is often between different provinces of the same kingdom. Men naturally flock to capital cities, seaports, and navigable rivers. There we find more men, more industry, more commodities, and consequently more money, but still the latter difference holds proportion with the former, and the level is preserved.

Our jealousy and our hatred of France are without bounds; and the former sentiment, at least, must be acknowledged reasonable and well-grounded. These passions have occasioned innumerable barriers and obstructions upon commerce, where we are accused of being commonly the aggressors. But what have we gained by the bargain? We lost the French market for our woolen manufactures, and transferred the commerce of wine to Spain and Portugal, where we buy worse liquor at a higher price. There are few Englishmen who would not think their country absolutely ruined, were French wines sold in England so cheap and in such abundance as to supplant, in some measure, all ale and home-brewed liquors: but would we lay aside prejudice, it would not be difficult to prove, that nothing could be more innocent, perhaps advantageous. Each new acre of vineyard planted in France, in order to supply England with wine, would make it requisite for the French to take the produce of an English acre, sown in wheat or barley, in order to subsist themselves; and it is evident that we should thereby get command of the better commodity. . . .

Mareschal Vauban complains often, and with reason, of the absurd duties which load the entry of those wines of Languedoc, Guienne, and other southern provinces, that are imported into Britany and Normandy. He entertained no doubt but these latter provinces could preserve their balance, notwithstanding the open commerce which he recommends. And it is evident, that a few leagues more navigation to England would make no difference; or if it did, that it must operate alike on the commodities of both kingdoms. . . .

. . . We fancy, because an individual would be much richer, were his stock of money doubled, that the same good effect would follow, were the money of every one increased; not considering that this would raise as much the price of every commodity, and reduce every man in time to the same condition as before. . . .

Before the introduction of paper money into our colonies, they had gold and silver sufficient for their circulation. Since the introduction of that commodity [paper money], the least inconveniency that has followed is the total banishment of the precious metals. And after the abolition of paper, can it be doubted but money will return, while those colonies possess manufactures and commodities, the only thing valuable in commerce, and for whose sake alone all men desire money?

What pity Lycurgus did not think of paper-credit, when he wanted to banish gold and silver from Sparta! It would have served his purpose better than the lumps of iron he made use of as money; and would also have prevented more effectually all commerce with strangers, as not being of so much real and intrinsic value. . . .

From these principles we may learn what judgment we ought to form of those numberless bars, obstructions, and imposts, which all nations of Europe, and none more than England, have put upon trade, from an exorbitant desire of amassing money, which never will heap up beyond its level, while it circulates; or from an ill-grounded apprehension of losing their specie, which never will sink below it. Could anything scatter our riches, it would be such impolitic contrivances. But this general ill effect, however, results from them, that they deprive neighboring nations of that free communication and exchange which the Author of the world has intended, by giving them soils, climates, and geniuses, so different from each other. . . .

. . . They adopt a hundred contrivances, which serve to no purpose but to check industry, and rob ourselves and our neighbors of the common benefits of art and nature.

. . . And as it is necessary that imposts should be levied for the support of government, it may be thought more convenient to lay them on foreign commodities, which can easily be intercepted at the port, and subjected to the impost. We ought, however, always to remember the maxim of Dr. Swift, that, in the arithmetic of the customs, two and two make not four, but often make only one. It can scarcely be doubted, but if the duties on wine were lowered to a third, they would yield much more to the government than at present. . . .

In short, a government has great reason to preserve with care its people and its manufactures. Its money, it may safely trust to the course of human affairs, without fear or jealousy. . . .

VI

Of Commerce

FOREIGN COMMERCE ... augment[s] ... the power of the state, as well as the riches and happiness of the subject. It increases the stock of labor in the nation; and the sovereign may convert what share of it he finds necessary to the service of the public. Foreign trade, by its imports, furnishes materials for new manufactures; and, by its exports, it produces labor in particular commodities, which could not be consumed at home. ...

If we consult history, we shall find, that in most nations foreign trade has preceded any refinement in home manufactures. ... This perhaps is the chief advantage which arises from a commerce with strangers. It rouses men from their indolence; and, presenting the gayer and more opulent part of the nation with objects of luxury which they never before dreamed of, raises in them a desire of a more splendid way of life than what their ancestors enjoyed. And at the same time, the few merchants who possessed the secret of this importation and exportation, make great profits, and, becoming rivals in wealth to the ancient nobility, tempt other adventurers to become their rivals in commerce. Imitation soon diffuses all those arts, while domestic manufacturers emulate the foreign in their improvements, and work up every home commodity to the utmost perfection of which it is susceptible. Their own steel and iron, in such laborious hands, become equal to the gold and rubies of the Indies. . . .

It will not, I hope, be considered as a superfluous digression, if I here observe, that as the multitude of mechanical arts is advantageous, so is the great number of persons to whose share the productions of these arts fall. A too great disproportion among the citizens weakens any state. Every person, if possible, ought to enjoy the fruits of his labor, in a full possession of all the necessaries, and many of the conveniences of life. . . .

Add to this, that where the riches are in few hands, these must enjoy all the power, and will readily conspire to lay the whole burden on the poor, and oppress them still further, to the discouragement of all industry. . . .

. . . The poverty of the common people is a natural, if not an infallible effect of absolute monarchy;

though I doubt whether it be always true on the other hand, that their riches are an infallible result of liberty. Liberty must be attended with particular accidents, and a certain turn of thinking, in order to produce that effect. . . .

VII

Of Public Credit

I‍T APPEARS TO have been the common practice of antiquity, to make provision, during peace, for the necessities of war, and to hoard up treasures beforehand as the instruments either of conquest or defense; without trusting to extraordinary impositions, much less to borrowing in times of disorder and confusion. . . .

On the contrary, our modern expedient, which has become very general, is to mortgage the public revenues, and to trust that posterity will pay off the encumbrances contracted by their ancestors: and they, having before their eyes so good an example of their wise fathers, have the same prudent reliance on *their* posterity; who, at last, from necessity more than choice, are obliged to place the same confidence in a new posterity.

But not to waste time in declaiming against a practice which appears ruinous beyond all controversy, it seems pretty apparent, that the ancient maxims are, in this respect, more prudent than the modern; even though the latter had been confined within some reasonable bounds, and had ever, in any instance, been attended with such frugality, in time of peace, as to discharge the debts incurred by an expensive war. For why should the case be so different between the public and an individual, as to make us establish different maxims of conduct for each? If the funds of the former be greater, its necessary expenses are proportionally larger; if its resources be more numerous, they are not infinite; and as its frame should be calculated for a much longer duration than the date of a single life, or even of a family, it should embrace maxims, large, durable, and generous, agreeably to the supposed extent of its existence.

To trust to chances and temporary expedients, is, indeed, what the necessity of human affairs frequently renders unavoidable; but whoever voluntarily depends on such resources, have not necessity, but their own folly to accuse for their misfortunes, when any such befall them.

If the abuses of treasures be dangerous, either by engaging the state in rash enterprises, or making it neglect military discipline, in confidence of its riches; the abuses of mortgaging are more certain and inevitable; poverty, impotence, and subjection to foreign powers. . . .

It is very tempting to a minister to employ such an expedient, as enables him to make a great figure during his administration, without overburdening the people with taxes, or exciting any immediate clamors against himself. The practice, therefore, of contracting debt, will almost infallibly be abused in every government. It would scarcely be more imprudent to give a prodigal son a credit in every banker's shop in London, than to empower a statesman to draw bills, in this manner, upon posterity.

What, then, shall we say to the new paradox, that public encumbrances are, of themselves, advantageous, independent of the necessity of contracting them. . . . Reasonings such as these might naturally have passed for trials of wit among rhetoricians, like the panegyrics on folly and fever, on Busiris and Nero, had we not seen such absurd maxims patronized by great ministers, and by a whole party among us. . . .

Public securities are with us become a kind of money, and pass as readily at the current price as gold or silver. . . . In short our national debts furnish merchants with a species of money that is continually multiplying in their hands, and produces sure gain, besides the profits of their commerce. . . .

. . . Were there no funds, great merchants would have no expedient for realizing or securing any part of their profit, but by making purchases of land; and land has many disadvantages in comparison of funds. Requiring more care and inspection, it divides the time and attention of the merchant: upon any tempting offer or extraordinary accident in trade, it is not so easily converted into money; and as it attracts too much, both by the many natural pleasures it affords, and the authority it gives, it soon converts the citizen into the country gentleman. More men, therefore, with large stocks and incomes, may naturally be supposed to continue in trade, where there are public debts; and this, it must be owned, is of some advantage to commerce, by diminishing its profits, promoting circulation, and encouraging industry.

But, in opposition to these two favorable circumstances, perhaps of no very great importance, weigh the many disadvantages which attend our public debts in the whole *interior* economy of the state: you will find no comparison between the ill and the good which result from them. . . .

We have indeed been told, that the public is no weaker on account of its debts, since they are mostly due among ourselves, and bring as much property to one as they take from another. It is like transferring money from the right hand to the left, which leaves the person neither richer nor poorer than before. Such loose reasoning and specious comparisons will always pass where we judge not upon principles. I ask,

"Is it possible, in the nature of things, to overburden a nation with taxes. . . . But if all our present taxes be mortgaged, must we not invent new ones? And may not this matter be carried to a length that is ruinous and destructive?" . . .

Suppose the public once fairly brought to that condition to which it is hastening with such amazing rapidity; suppose the land to be taxed eighteen or nineteen shillings in the pound, for it can never bear the whole twenty; suppose all the excises and customs to be screwed up to the utmost which the nation can bear, without entirely losing its commerce and industry; and suppose that all those funds are mortgaged to perpetuity, and that the invention and wit of all our projectors can find no new imposition which may serve as the foundation of a new loan; and let us consider the necessary consequences of this situation. Though the imperfect state of our political knowledge, and the narrow capacities of men, make it difficult to foretell the effects which will result from any untried measure, the seeds of ruin are here scattered with such profusion as not to escape the eye of the most careless observer. . . .

Though a resolution should be formed by the legislature never to impose any tax which hurts commerce and discourages industry, it will be impossible for men, in subjects of such extreme delicacy, to reason so justly as never to be mistaken, or, amidst difficulties so urgent, never to be seduced from their resolution. . . . And any great blow given to trade, whether by injudicious taxes or by other accidents, throws the whole system of government into confusion. . . .

. . . It must, indeed, be one of these two events; either the nation must destroy public credit, or public credit will destroy the nation. It is impossible that they can both subsist. . . .

. . . He asserted that there was a fallacy in imagining that the public owed this debt; for that really every individual owed a proportional share of it, and paid, in his taxes, a proportional share of the interest, besides the expense of levying these taxes. . . . It is not altogether improbable, that when the nation becomes heartily sick of their debts, and is cruelly oppressed by them, some daring projector may arise with visionary schemes for their discharge. And as public credit will begin, by that time, to be a little frail, the least touch will destroy it, as happened in France during the regency; and in this manner it will *die of the doctor*. . . .

. . . The funds, created and mortgaged, will by that time bring in a large yearly revenue, sufficient for the defense and security of the nation: money is perhaps lying in the exchequer, ready for the discharge of the quarterly interest: necessity calls, fear urges, reason exhorts, compassion alone exclaims: the money will immediately be seized for the current service, under the most solemn protestations, perhaps of being immediately replaced. But no more is requisite. The whole fabric, already tottering, falls to the ground, and buries thousands in its ruins. And this, I think, may be called the *natural death* of public credit; for to this period it tends as naturally as an animal body to its dissolution and destruction.

So great dupes are the generality of mankind, that notwithstanding such a violent shock to public credit, as a voluntary bankruptcy in England would occasion, it would not probably be long ere credit would again revive in as flourishing a condition as before. The present king of France, during the late war, borrowed money at a lower interest than ever his grandfather did; and as low as the British parliament, comparing the natural rate of interest in both kingdoms. And though men are commonly more governed by what they have seen, than by what they foresee, with whatever certainty; yet promises, protestations, fair appearances, with the allurements of present interest, have such powerful influence as few are able to resist. Mankind are, in all ages, caught by the same baits: the same tricks played over and over again, still trepan them.

The heights of popularity and patriotism are still the beaten road to power and tyranny; flattery, to treachery; standing armies to arbitrary government; and the glory of God to the temporal interest of the clergy. The fear of an everlasting destruction of credit, allowing it to be an evil, is a needless bugbear. A prudent man, in reality, would rather lend to the public immediately after we had taken a sponge to our debts, than at present; as much as an opulent knave, even though one could not force *him* to pay, is a preferable debtor to an honest bankrupt: for the former, in order to carry on business, may find it his interest to discharge his debts, where they are not exorbitant: the latter has it not in his power.... The public is a debtor, whom no man can oblige to pay. The only check which the creditors have upon her, is the interest of preserving credit; an interest which may easily be overbalanced by a great debt, and by a difficult and extraordinary emergence, even supposing that credit irrecoverable....

These seem to be the events, which are not very remote, and which reason foresees as clearly almost as she can do anything that lies in the womb of time. And though the ancients maintained, that in order to reach the gift of prophecy, a certain divine fury or madness was requisite, one may safely affirm, that in order to deliver such prophecies as these, no more is necessary than merely to be in one's senses, free from the influence of popular madness and delusion.

VIII

Of Taxes

THE BEST TAXES are such as are levied upon consumptions, especially those of luxury; because such taxes are least felt by the people. They seem, in some measure, voluntary; since a man may choose how far he will use the commodity which is taxed. . . . Their only disadvantage is, that they are expensive in the levying. . . .

IX

Of the Populousness of Ancient Nations
(Slavery in the Ancient World)

T HE REMAINS WHICH are found of domestic slavery, in the American colonies, and
among some European nations, would never
surely create a desire of rendering it more universal.
The little humanity commonly observed in persons
accustomed, from their infancy, to exercise so great
authority over their fellow-creatures, and to trample
upon human nature, were sufficient alone to disgust
us with that unbounded dominion. . . .

The custom of exposing old, useless, or sick slaves in
a stand of the Tiber, there to starve, seems to have been

pretty common in Rome; and whoever recovered, after having been so exposed, had his liberty given him by an edict of the Emperor Claudius; in which it was likewise forbidden to kill any slave merely for old age or sickness. But supposing that this edict was strictly obeyed, would it better the domestic treatment of slaves, or render their lives much more comfortable? We may imagine what others would practice, when it was the professed maxim of the elder Cato, to sell his superannuated slaves for any price, rather than maintain what he esteemed a useless burden. . . .

[There was] nothing so common in all trials, even of civil causes, as to call for the evidence of slaves; which was always extorted by the most exquisite torments. Demosthenes says, that, where it was possible to produce, for the same fact, either freemen or slaves, as witnesses, the judges always preferred the torturing of slaves as a more certain evidence.

Seneca draws a picture of that disorderly luxury which changes day into night, and night into day, and inverts every stated hour of every office in life. Among other circumstances, such as displacing the meals and times of bathing, he mentions, that, regularly about the third hour of the night, the neighbors of one, who indulges this false refinement, hear the noise of whips and lashes; and, upon inquiry, find that he is then taking an account of the conduct of his servants, and giving them due correction and discipline. This is not remarked as an instance of cruelty, but only of disorder, which, even in actions the most usual and methodical, changes the fixed hours that an established custom had assigned for them. . . .

Consider this passage of Plutarch, speaking of the Elder Cato:

> He had a great number of slaves, whom he took care to buy at the sales of prisoners of war; and he chose them young, that they might easily be accustomed to any diet or manner of life, and be instructed in any business or labor, as men teach anything to young dogs or horses. And esteeming love the chief source of all disorders, he allowed the male slaves to have a commerce with the female in his family, upon paying a certain sum for this privilege: but he strictly prohibited all intrigues out of his family. . . .

History mentions a Roman nobleman who had 400 slaves under the same roof with him: and having been assassinated at home by the furious revenge of one of them, the law was executed with rigor, and all without exception were put to death. . . .

The practice, indeed, of marrying slaves, seems not to have been very common, even among the country laborers, where it is more naturally to be expected. Cato, enumerating the slaves requisite to labor a vineyard of a hundred acres, makes them amount to 15; the overseer and his wife, *villicus* and *villica,* and 13 male slaves; for an olive plantation of 240 acres, the overseer and his wife, and 11 male slaves; and so in proportion to a greater or less plantation or vineyard....

... All I pretend to infer from these reasonings is, that slavery is in general disadvantageous both to the happiness and populousness of mankind, and that its place is much better supplied by the practice of hired servants....

X

Of Government

That Politics May Be Reduced to a Science

IT IS A question with several, whether there be any essential difference between one form of government and another and, whether every form may not become good or bad, according as it is well or ill administered? . . .

But here it may be proper to make a distinction. All absolute governments must very much depend on the administration; and this is one of the great inconveniences attending that form of government.

Legislators, therefore, ought not to trust the future government of a state entirely to chance, but ought to provide a system of laws to regulate the administration of public affairs. . . .

. . . Good laws may beget order and moderation in the government, where the manners and customs have instilled little humanity or justice into the tempers of men. . . .

Of the Origin of Government

We are . . . to look upon all the vast apparatus of our government, as having ultimately no other object or purpose but the distribution of justice. . . .

All men are sensible of the necessity of justice to maintain peace and order; and all men are sensible of the necessity of peace and order for the maintenance of society. . . . But much more frequently he is seduced from his great and important, but distant interests, by the allurement of present, though often very frivolous temptations. This great weakness is incurable in human nature.

Men must, therefore, endeavor to palliate what they cannot cure. They must institute some persons under the appellation of magistrates, whose peculiar office it is to point out the decrees of equity, to punish transgressors, to correct fraud and violence, and to oblige men, however reluctant, to consult their own real and permanent interests. In a word, obedience is a new duty which must be invented to support that of justice. . . .

In all governments, there is a perpetual intestine struggle, open or secret, between authority and liberty; and neither of them can ever absolutely prevail in the contest. . . . The government, which, in common appellation, receives the appellation of free, is that which admits of a partition of power among several members, whose united authority is no less, or is commonly greater, than that of any monarch; but who, in the usual course of administration, must act by general and equal laws, that are previously known to all the members, and to all their subjects. . . .

Of Civil Liberty

. . . Trade was never esteemed an affair of state till the last century; and there scarcely is any ancient writer on politics who has made mention of it. . . .

The source of degeneracy which may be remarked in free governments, consists in the practice of contracting debt, and mortgaging the public revenues, by which taxes may, in time, become altogether intolerable. . . . The practice is of modern date.

Of the Rise and Progress of the Arts and Sciences

. . . The desire of gain, is a universal passion, which operates at all times, in all places, and upon all persons:

but curiosity, or the love of knowledge, has a very limited influence, and requires youth, leisure, education, genius, and example, to make it govern any person.…

My first observation on this head is, *That it is impossible for the arts and sciences to arise, at first, among any people, unless that people enjoy the blessing of a free government.*

In the first ages of the world, when men are as yet barbarous and ignorant, they seek no further security against mutual violence and injustice than the choice of some rulers, few or many, in whom they place an implicit confidence, without providing any security, by laws or political institutions, against the violence and injustice of these rulers.…

A people, governed after such a manner, are slaves in the full and proper sense of the word; and it is impossible they can ever aspire to any refinements of taste or reason. They dare not so much as pretend to enjoy the necessaries of life in plenty or security.…

To expect, therefore, that the arts and sciences should take their first rise in a monarchy, is to expect a contradiction. Before these refinements have taken place, the monarch is ignorant and uninstructed; and not having knowledge sufficient to make him sensible of the necessity of balancing his government upon general laws, he delegates his full power to all inferior magistrates. This barbarous policy debases the people, and forever prevents all improvements.…

Here then are the advantages of free states. Though a republic should be barbarous, it necessarily, by an infallible operation, gives rise to law, even before mankind have made any considerable advances in the other sciences. From law arises security; from security curiosity; and from curiosity knowledge. . . .

The next observation which I shall make on this head is, *That nothing is more favorable to the rise of politeness and learning, than a number of neighboring and independent states, connected together by commerce and policy.* The emulation which naturally arises among those neighboring states is an obvious source of improvement. But what I would chiefly insist on is the stop which such limited territories give both to *power* and to *authority*. . . .

Extended governments, where a single person has great influence, soon become absolute; but small ones change naturally into commonwealths. A large government is accustomed by degrees to tyranny, because each act of violence is at first performed upon a part, which, being distant from the majority, is not taken notice of, nor excites any violent ferment. . . .

The divisions into small states are favorable to learning, by stopping the progress of *authority* as well as that of *power*. Reputation is often as great a fascination upon men as sovereignty, and is equally destructive to the freedom of thought and examination. But where a number of neighboring states have a great intercourse of arts and commerce, their mutual jealousy keeps them from receiving too lightly the law from each other, in matters of taste and of reasoning, and makes them examine every work of art with the greatest care and accuracy. The contagion of popular opinion spreads not so easily from one place to another. It readily receives a check in some state or other, where it concurs not with the prevailing prejudices. And nothing but nature and reason, or at least what bears them a strong resemblance, can force its way through all obstacles, and unite the most rival nations into an esteem and admiration of it.

Greece was a cluster of little principalities, which soon became republics; and being united both by their near neighborhood, and by the ties of the same language and interest, they entered into the closest intercourse of commerce and learning. There concurred a happy climate, a soil not unfertile, and a most harmonious and comprehensive language; so that every circumstance among that people seemed to favor the rise of the arts and sciences. . . .

Europe is at present a copy, at large, of what Greece was formerly a pattern in miniature. . . . The severest scrutiny which Newton's theory has undergone proceeded not from his own countrymen, but from foreigners; and if it can overcome the obstacles which it meets with at present in all parts of Europe, it will probably go down triumphant to the latest posterity. . . .

I have sometimes been inclined to think, that interruptions in the periods of learning, were they not attended with such a destruction of ancient books, and the records of history, would be rather favorable to the arts and sciences, by breaking the progress of authority, and dethroning the tyrannical usurpers over human reason, have attempted to gain an ascendant over them.....

The *third* observation, which I shall form on this head, of the rise and progress of the arts and sciences, is, *That, though the only proper* nursery *of these noble plants be a free state, yet may they be transplanted into any government; and that a republic is most favorable to the growth of the sciences, and a civilized monarchy to that of the polite arts.*

To balance a large state or society, whether monarchical or republican, on general laws, is a work of so great difficulty, that no human genius, however comprehensive, is able, by the mere dint of reason and reflection, to effect it. The judgments of many must unite in this work: experience must guide their labor: time must bring it to perfection: and the feeling of inconveniences must correct the mistakes, which they inevitably fall into, in their first trials and experiments.....

But though law, the source of all security and happiness, arises late in any government, and is the slow product of order and of liberty, it is not preserved with the same difficulty with which it is produced;

but when it has once taken root, is a hardy plant, which will scarcely ever perish through the ill culture of men, or the rigor of the seasons.

The arts of luxury, and much more the liberal arts, which depend on a refined taste or sentiment, are easily lost; because they are always relished by a few only, whose leisure, fortune, and genius, fit them for such amusements. . . .

Among the arts of conversation, no one pleases more than mutual deference or civility, which leads us to resign our own inclinations to those of our companion, and to curb and conceal that presumption and arrogance so natural to the human mind. A good-natured man, who is well educated, practices this civility to every mortal, without premeditation or interest. But in order to render that valuable quality general among any people, it seems necessary to assist the natural disposition by some general motive.

Where power rises upwards from the people to the great, as in all republics, such refinements of civility are apt to be little practiced, since the whole state is, by that means, brought near to a level, and every member of it is rendered, in a great measure, independent of another. The people have the advantage, by the authority of their suffrages; the great by the superiority of their station. But in a civilized monarchy, there is a long train of dependence from the prince to the peasant, which is not great enough to render property precarious, or depress the minds of the people; but is sufficient to beget in every one an inclination to please his superiors, and to form himself upon those models which are most acceptable to people of condition and education. Politeness of manners, therefore, arises most naturally in monarchies and courts; and where that flourishes, none of the liberal arts will be altogether neglected or despised. . . .

Of Some Remarkable Customs

. . . As long as men are actuated by the passions of ambition, emulation, and avarice, which have hitherto been their chief governing principles . . . , it is a maxim in politics, which we readily admit as undisputed and universal, that a power, however great, when granted by law to an eminent magistrate, is not so dangerous to liberty as an authority, however inconsiderable, which he acquires from violence and usurpation. For besides that the law always limits every power which it bestows, the very receiving it as a concession establishes the authority whence it is derived, and preserves the harmony of the constitution. By the same right that one prerogative is assumed without law, another may also be claimed, and another, with still greater facility; while the first usurpations both serve as precedents to the following, and give force to maintain them. Hence the heroism of Hampden's conduct, who sustained the whole violence of royal prosecution, rather than pay a tax of twenty shillings not imposed by parliament; hence the care of all English patriots to guard against the first encroachments of the crown; and hence alone the existence, at this day, of English liberty. . . .

Of the Protestant Succession (On Political Tactics)

. . . Reserve or disguise . . . are always employed by those who enter upon any new project, or endeavor to innovate in any government. . . .

Part Four

Life

A Treatise of Human Nature

(1738)

Book I

Section XII

I AM FIRST AFFRIGHTED and confounded with that forlorn solitude, in which I am placed in my philosophy, and fancy myself some strange uncouth monster, who not being able to mingle and unite in society, has been expelled all human commerce, and left utterly abandoned and disconsolate. Fain would I run into the crowd for shelter and warmth; but cannot prevail with myself to mix with such deformity. I call upon others to join me, in order to make a company apart; but no one will hearken to me. Everyone keeps at a distance, and dreads that storm, which beats upon me from every side. I have exposed myself to the enmity of all metaphysicians, logicians, mathematicians, and even theologians; and can I wonder at the insults I must suffer? I have declared my disapprobation of their systems; and can I be surprised, if they should express a hatred of mine and of my person? When I look abroad, I foresee on every side, dispute, contradiction, anger, calumny and detraction. When I turn my eye inward, I find nothing but doubt and ignorance. All the world conspires to oppose and contradict me; though such is my weakness, that I feel all my opinions loosen and fall of themselves, when unsupported by the approbation of others. Every step I take is with hesitation, and every new reflection makes me dread an error and absurdity in my reasoning. . . .

Most fortunately it happens, that since reason is incapable of dispelling these clouds, nature herself suffices to that purpose, and cures me of this philosophical melancholy and delirium, either by relaxing this bent of mind, or by some avocation, and lively impression of my senses, which obliterate all these chimeras. I dine, I play a game of backgammon, I converse, and am merry with my friends; and when after three or four hours' amusement, I would return to these speculations, they appear so cold, and strained, and ridiculous, that I cannot find in my heart to enter into them any farther. . . .

[But] at the time . . . that I am tired with amusement and company, and have indulged a reverie in my chamber, or in a solitary walk by a riverside, I feel my mind all collected within itself, and am naturally inclined to carry my view into all those subjects, about which I have met with so many disputes in the course of my reading and conversation. I cannot forbear having a curiosity to be acquainted with the principles of moral good and evil, the nature and foundation of government, and the cause of those several passions and inclinations, which actuate and govern me. I am uneasy to think I approve of one object, and disapprove of another; call one thing beautiful, and another deformed; decide concerning truth and falsehood, reason and folly, without knowing upon what principles I proceed. I am concerned for the condition of the learned world, which lies under such deplorable ignorance in all these particulars. I feel an ambition to arise in me of contributing to the instruction of mankind, and of acquiring a name by my inventions and discoveries. These sentiments spring up naturally in my present disposition; and should I endeavor to banish them, by attaching myself to any other business or diversion, I feel I should be a loser in point of pleasure; and this is the origin of my philosophy.

But even suppose this curiosity and ambition should not transport me into speculations without the sphere of common life, it would necessarily happen, that from my very weakness I must be led into such enquiries. It is certain, that superstition is much more bold in its systems and hypotheses than philosophy; and while the latter contents itself with assigning new causes and principles to the phenomena, which appear in the visible world, the former opens a world of its own, and presents us with scenes, and beings, and objects, which are altogether new. Since therefore it is almost impossible for the mind of man to rest, like those of beasts, in that narrow circle of objects, which are the subject of daily conversation and action, we ought only to deliberate concerning the choice of our guide, and ought to prefer that which is safest and most agreeable. And in this respect I make bold to recommend philosophy, and shall not scruple to give it the preference to superstition of every kind or denomination. For as superstition arises naturally and easily from the popular opinions of mankind, it seizes more strongly on the mind, and is often able to disturb us in the conduct of our lives and actions. Philosophy on the contrary, if just, can present us only with mild and moderate sentiments; and if false and extravagant, its opinions are merely the objects of a cold and general speculation, and seldom go so far as to interrupt the course of our natural propensities. The Cynics are an extraordinary instance of philosophers, who from reasonings purely philosophical ran into as great extravagancies of conduct as any Monk or Dervish that ever was in the world. Generally speaking, the errors in religion are dangerous; those in philosophy only ridiculous.

I am sensible, that these two cases of the strength and weakness of the mind will not comprehend all mankind, and that there are in England, in particular, many honest gentlemen, who being always employed in their domestic affairs, or amusing themselves in common recreations, have carried their thoughts very little beyond those objects, which are every day exposed to their senses. And indeed, of such as these I pretend not to make philosophers, nor do I expect them either to be associates in these researches or auditors of these discoveries. They do well to keep themselves in their present situation; and instead of refining them into philosophers, I wish we could communicate to our founders of systems, a share of this gross earthy mixture, as an ingredient, which they commonly stand much in need of. . . .

The Life of David Hume, Esq.
(Written by Himself)

My Own Life

I RESOLVED TO MAKE a very rigid frugality supply my deficiency of fortune, to maintain unimpaired my independency, and to regard every object as contemptible, except the improvement of my talents in literature. . . .

. . . I was now master of near a thousand pounds.

. . . On my return from Italy, I had the mortification to find all England in a ferment, on account of Dr. Middleton's Free Enquiry, while my performance was entirely overlooked and neglected. . . .

. . . However, I had fixed a resolution, which I inflexibly maintained, never to reply to anybody; and not being very irascible in my temper, I have easily kept myself clear of all literary squabbles. These symptoms of a rising reputation gave me encouragement, as I was ever more disposed to see the favorable than unfavorable side of things; a turn of mind which it is more happy to possess, than to be born to an estate of ten thousand a year.

In 1751, I removed from the country to the town, the true scene for a man of letters. In 1752, were published at Edinburgh, where I then lived, my *Political Discourses*, the only work of mine that was successful on the first publication. It was well received abroad and at home. In the same year was published at London, my *Enquiry Concerning the Principles of Morals*; which, in my own opinion (who ought not to judge on that subject), is of all my writings, historical, philosophical, or literary, incomparably the best. It came unnoticed and unobserved into the world. . . .

. . . Mr. Millar told me, that in a twelve-month he sold only forty-five copies of it. . . .

I was . . . , I confess, discouraged; and had not the war been at that time breaking out between France and England, I had certainly retired to some provincial town of the former kingdom, have changed my name, and never more have returned to my native country. But as this scheme was not now practicable, and the subsequent volume was considerably advanced, I resolved to pick up courage and to persevere. . . .

. . . I retired to my native country of Scotland, determined never more to set my foot out of it; and retaining the satisfaction of never having preferred a request to one great man, or even making advances of friendship to any of them. . . . This offer [to be companion and tutor to a noble young man], however inviting, I at first declined, both because I was reluctant to begin connections with the great, and because I was afraid that the civilities and gay company of Paris, would prove disagreeable to a person of my age and humor: but on his lordship's repeating the invitation, I accepted of it. . . .

I was appointed secretary to the embassy [at Paris]; and, in summer 1765, Lord Hertford left me, being appointed Lord Lieutenant of Ireland. I was *chargé d'affaires* till the arrival of the Duke of Richmond, towards the end of the year. . . . I returned to Edinburgh in 1768, very opulent (for I possessed a revenue of £1000 a year), healthy, and though somewhat stricken in years, with the prospect of enjoying long my ease, and of seeing the increase of my reputation. . . .

. . . I possess the same ardor as ever in study, and the same gaiety in company. . . . It is difficult to be more detached from life than I am at present. . . .

. . . I was, I say, a man of mild dispositions, of command of temper, of an open, social, and cheerful humor, capable of attachment, but little susceptible of enmity, and of great moderation in all my passions. . . .

April 18, 1776

Letter from Adam Smith, LLD, to William Strahan, Esq.

Kirkaldy, Fifeshire
November 9, 1776

Dear Sir,

It is with a real, though a very melancholy pleasure, that I sit down to give you some account of the behavior of our late excellent friend, Mr. Hume, during his last illness.

Though, in his own judgment, his disease was mortal and incurable, yet he allowed himself to be prevailed upon, by the entreaty of his friends, to try what might be the effects of a long journey. A few days before he set out, he wrote that account of his own life, which, together with his other papers, he has left to your care. My account, therefore, shall begin where his ends.

He set out for London towards the end of April, and at Morpeth met with Mr. John Home and myself, who had both come down from London on purpose to see him, expecting to have found him at Edinburgh. Mr. Home returned with him, and attended him during the whole of his stay in England, with that care and attention which might be expected from a temper so perfectly friendly and affectionate. As I had written to my mother that she might expect me in Scotland, I was under the necessity of continuing my journey. His disease seemed to yield to exercise and change of air, and when he arrived in London, he was apparently in much better health than when he left Edinburgh. He was advised to go to Bath to drink the waters, which appeared for some time to have so good an effect upon him, that even he himself began to entertain, what he was not apt to do, a better opinion of his own health. His symptoms, however, soon returned with their usual violence, and from that moment he gave up all thoughts of recovery, but submitted with the utmost cheerfulness, and the most perfect complacency and resignation. Upon his return to Edinburgh, though he found himself much weaker, yet his cheerfulness never abated, and he continued to divert himself, as usual, with correcting his own works for a new edition, with reading books of amusement, with the conversation of his friends; and, sometimes in the evening, with a party at his favorite game of whist. His cheerfulness was so great, and his conversation and amusements run so much in their usual strain, that, notwithstanding all bad symptoms, many people could not believe he was dying. "I shall tell your friend, Colonel Edmondstone," said Doctor Dundas to him one day, "that I left you much better, and in a fair way of recovery." "Doctor," said he, "as I believe you would not chose to tell anything but the truth, you had better tell him, that I am dying as fast as my enemies, if I have any, could wish, and as easily and cheerfully as my best friends could desire." Colonel Edmondstone soon afterwards came to see him, and take leave of him; and on his way home, he could not forbear writing him a letter bidding him once more an eternal adieu, and applying to him, as to a dying man, the beautiful French verses in which the Abbe Chaulieu, in expectation of his own death, laments his approaching separation from his friend, the Marquis de la Fare. Mr. Hume's magnanimity and firmness were such, that his most affectionate friends knew, that they hazarded nothing in talking or writing to him as to a dying man, and that so far from being hurt by this frankness, he was rather pleased and flattered by it. I happened to come into his room while he was reading this letter, which he had just received, and which he immediately showed me. I told him, that though I was sensible how very much he was weakened, and that appearances were in many respects very bad, yet his cheerfulness was still so great, the spirit of life seemed still to be so very strong in him, that I could not help entertaining some faint hopes. He answered, "Your hopes are groundless. An habitual diarrhea of more than a year's standing, would be a very bad disease at any age: at my age it is a mortal one. When I lie down in the evening, I feel myself weaker than when I rose in the morning; and when I rise in the morning, weaker than when I lay down in the evening. I am sensible, besides, that some of my vital parts are affected, so that I must soon die." "Well," said I, "if it must be so, you have at least the satisfaction of leaving all your friends, your brother's family in particular, in great prosperity." He said that he felt that satisfaction so sensibly, that when he was reading a few days before, Lucian's *Dialogues of the Dead*, among all the excuses which are alleged to Charon for not entering readily into his boat, he could not find one that fitted him; he had no house to finish, he had no daughter to provide for, he had no enemies upon whom he wished to revenge himself. "I could not well imagine," said he, "what excuse I could make to Charon in order to obtain a little delay. I have done everything of consequence which I ever meant to do, and I could at no time expect to leave my relations and friends in a better situation than that in which I am now likely to leave them; I, therefore, have all reason to die contented." He then diverted himself with inventing several jocular excuses, which he supposed he might make to Charon, and with imagining the very surly answers which it might suit the character of Charon to return to them. "Upon further consideration," said he, "I thought I might say to him, 'Good Charon, I have been correcting my works for a new edition. Allow me a little time, that I may see how the Public receives the alterations.' But Charon would answer, 'When you have seen the effect of these, you will be for making other alterations. There will be no end of such excuses; so, honest friend, please step into the boat.' But I might still urge, 'Have a little patience, good Charon, I have been endeavoring to open the eyes of the Public. If I live a few years longer, I may have the satisfaction of seeing the downfall of some of the prevailing systems of superstition.' But Charon would then lose all temper and decency. 'You loitering rogue, that will not happen these many hundred years. Do you fancy I will grant you a lease for so long a term? Get into the boat this instant, you lazy loitering rogue.'"

But, though Mr. Hume always talked of his approaching dissolution with great cheerfulness, he never affected to make any parade of his magnanimity. He never mentioned the subject but when the conversation naturally led to it, and never dwelt longer upon it than the course of the conversation happened to require: it was a subject indeed which occurred pretty frequently, in consequence of the inquiries which his friends, who came to see him, naturally made concerning the state of his health. The conversation which I mentioned above, and which passed on Thursday the 8th of August, was the last, except one, that I ever had with him. He had now become so very weak, that the company of his most intimate friends fatigued him; for his cheerfulness was still so great, his complaisance and social disposition were still so entire, that when any friend was with him, he could not help talking more, and with greater exertion, than suited the weakness of his body. At his own desire, therefore, I agreed to leave Edinburgh, where I was staying partly upon his account, and returned to my mother's house here, at Kirkaldy, upon condition that he would send for me whenever he wished to see me; the physician who saw him most frequently, Doctor Black, undertaking, in the meantime, to write me occasionally an account of the state of his health.

On the 22nd of August, the Doctor wrote me the following letter:

Since my last, Mr. Hume has passed his time pretty easily, but is much weaker. He sits up, goes down stairs once a day, and amuses himself with reading, but seldom sees anybody. He finds that even the conversation of his most intimate friends fatigues and oppresses him; and it is happy that he does not need it, for he is quite free from anxiety, impatience, or low spirits, and passes his time very well with the assistance of amusing books.

I received the day after a letter from Mr. Hume himself, of which the following is an extract.

Edinburgh
23rd August, 1776

My Dearest Friend,

I am obliged to make use of my nephew's hand in writing to you, as I do not rise today. . . .

I go very fast to decline, and last night had a small fever, which I hoped might put a quicker period to this tedious illness, but unluckily it has, in a great measure, gone off. I cannot submit to your coming over here on my account, as it is possible for me to see you so small a part of the day, but Doctor Black can better inform you concerning the degree of strength which may from time to time remain with me.

Adieu, etc.

Three days after I received the following letter from Doctor Black:

Edinburgh
Monday, 26th August, 1776

Dear Sir,

Yesterday about four o'clock afternoon, Mr. Hume expired. The near approach of his death became evident in the night between Thursday and Friday, when his disease became excessive, and soon weakened him so much, that he could no longer rise out of his bed. He continued to the last perfectly sensible, and free from much pain or feelings of distress. He never dropped the smallest expression of impatience; but when he had occasion to speak to the people about him, always did it with affection and tenderness. I thought it improper to write to bring you over, especially as I heard that he had dictated a letter to you desiring you not to come. When he became very weak, it cost him an effort to speak, and he died in such a happy composure of mind, that nothing could exceed it.

Thus died our most excellent, and never to be forgotten friend; concerning whose philosophical opinions men will, no doubt, judge variously, every one approving, or condemning them, according as they happen to coincide or disagree with his own; but concerning whose character and conduct there can scarce be a difference of opinion. His temper, indeed, seemed to be more happily balanced, if I may be allowed such an expression, than that perhaps of any other man I have ever known. Even in the lowest state of his fortune, his great and necessary frugality never hindered him from exercising, upon proper occasions, acts both of charity and generosity. It was a frugality founded, not upon avarice, but upon the love of independency. The extreme gentleness of his nature never weakened either the firmness of his mind, or the steadiness of his resolutions. His constant pleasantry was the genuine effusion of good-nature and good-humor, tempered with delicacy and modesty, and without even the slightest tincture of malignity, so frequently the disagreeable source of what is called wit in other men. It never was the meaning of his raillery to mortify; and therefore, far from offending, it seldom failed to please and delight, even those who were the objects of it. To his friends, who were frequently the objects of it, there was not perhaps any one of all his great and amiable qualities, which contributed more to endear his conversation. And that gaiety of temper, so agreeable in society, but which is so often accompanied with frivolous and superficial qualities, was in him certainly attended with the most severe application, the most extensive learning, the greatest depth of thought, and a capacity in every respect the most comprehensive. Upon the whole, I have always considered him, both in his lifetime and since his death, as approaching as nearly to the idea of a perfectly wise and virtuous man, as perhaps the nature of human frailty will permit.

I ever am, dear Sir,
Most affectionately yours,
ADAM SMITH

Index